PRAISE FOR *BRAIN*

"A genuine breakthrough in accessing your brain's immense potential."
— Dr. Susan Raeburn, coauthor of *Creative Recovery*

"I sing, I write, I teach, I coach. In everything I do I need to go deeply into the work and also sustain it over time. *Brainstorm* is the first book to spell out how a person with multiple paths can pay real attention to everything! The information is invaluable."
— Darby Dizard, award-winning jazz singer and creator of the CD *Down for You*

"What's the process like for an actor who wants to keep a role fresh for the duration of a long-running play? It is exactly what Eric Maisel describes in these pages: the harnessing of a productive obsession! Maisel has articulated something that actors know but haven't had words for before."
— Ed Hooks, author of *The Actor's Field Guide*

"As the executive director of a nonprofit and as a working novelist, I have to get my mind to concentrate quickly on different — and equally important — trains of thought. Until *Brainstorm*, no one has explained how to get your mind to function this efficiently. For anyone who needs to focus, this is the book!"
— Roccie Hill, author of *Three Minutes on Love*

"As a science writer and student of scientific innovation, I fully appreciate Dr. Maisel's groundbreaking work on the way that big ideas really come into existence. Every scientist and fan of science should get their hands on *Brainstorm*!"
— John Moir, author of *Return of the Condor*

"Dr. Maisel precisely outlines the ways in which things like songs and symphonies spring into existence. Productive obsessions are the powerhouses of the creative process, and no one has described them like this before."
— Gerald Klickstein, author of *The Musician's Way*

"The brain may be the most complicated bit of matter in the universe, but that doesn't mean we can't get a grip on it and use it for our purposes. *Brainstorm* presents a new way of thinking about how to turn brain potential into passion, energy, and genuine accomplishments."
— Camille Minichino, physicist and author of the Periodic Table Mysteries

FROM REVIEWS OF ERIC MAISEL'S PREVIOUS BOOKS

"Eric Maisel has made a career out of helping artists cope with the traumas and troubles that are the price of admission to a creative life."
— *Intuition* magazine

"Eric Maisel's psychological approach sets his work apart."
— *Library Journal*

"Eric Maisel's books should be required reading for anyone involved in the arts."
— *Theatre Design and Technology Journal*

"Eric Maisel is a meticulous guide who knows the psychological landscape that artists inhabit."
— *The Writer* magazine

brainstorm

ALSO BY ERIC MAISEL

NONFICTION

Affirmations for Artists
The Art of the Book Proposal
The Atheist's Way
Coaching the Artist Within
Creative Recovery
The Creativity Book
Creativity for Life
Deep Writing
Everyday You
Fearless Creating
A Life in the Arts
Living the Writer's Life
Performance Anxiety
Sleep Thinking
Ten Zen Seconds
Toxic Criticism
20 Communication Tips at Work
20 Communication Tips for Families
The Van Gogh Blues
What Would Your Character Do?
Write Mind
A Writer's Paris
A Writer's San Francisco
A Writer's Space

FICTION

The Blackbirds of Mulhouse
The Black Narc
Dismay
The Fretful Dancer
The Kingston Papers

JOURNALS

Artists Speak
Writers and Artists on Devotion
Writers and Artists on Love

MEDITATION DECKS

Everyday Calm
Everyday Creative
Everyday Smart

E-BOOKS

Becoming a Creativity Coach
The Power of Sleep Thinking

HOME STUDY COURSE

The Meaning Solution

brainstorm

Harnessing the Power
of Productive Obsessions

Eric Maisel, PhD
and Ann Maisel

New World Library
Novato, California

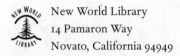 New World Library
14 Pamaron Way
Novato, California 94949

Text design by Tona Pearce Myers

Library of Congress Cataloging-in-Publication Data
Maisel, Eric, date.
Brainstorm : harnessing the power of productive obsessions / Eric Maisel and
Ann Maisel.
  p. cm.
Includes bibliographical references and index.
ISBN 978-1-57731-621-3 (pbk. : alk. paper)
  1. Brainstorming. 2. Creative thinking. 3. Creative ability in business. I. Maisel,
Ann, date. II. Title.
BF408.M23195 2010
153.3'5—dc22   2010008274

First printing, June 2010
ISBN 978-1-57731-621-3
Printed in Canada on 100% postconsumer-waste recycled paper

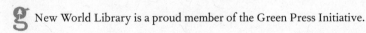 New World Library is a proud member of the Green Press Initiative.

10 9 8 7 6 5 4 3 2 1

Contents

Introduction

I N THIS BOOK I'M GOING TO DESCRIBE a wonderful habit of mind that's available to you right now. When you get into the habit of biting more fully into your own ideas, stirring up brainstorms, and productively obsessing, you feel more alive and become more creative. You do a better job of solving your problems. You give your brain the gift of a productive obsession by inviting it to think hard about something that matters to you, and your brain thanks you, having been waiting for exactly that invitation. These brainstorms are one of the brain's glories, and this invitation is the only gift your brain has ever really wanted.

I want to explain to you both the virtues and the practicalities of brainstorms: why you want to cultivate productive obsessions, what makes them so powerful, and how to nurture and use them. In addition to my own observations as a creativity coach, meaning coach, and family therapist, I'll include observations from real people who have participated in the cyberspace productive obsession group that I run. They do not have only rosy stories to tell; like you, they begin the process unsure of what to obsess about or why to obsess, doubtful that they have it in them to nurture large ideas or to see them to fruition, and as ready to quit as to proceed. But many of them do persevere, and I think you will find it interesting to see what they learn and what they accomplish.

This book connects to certain ideas that I've presented previously. In *The Van Gogh Blues* I explained that an intimate relationship exists between creativity and existential depression. I argued that "making meaning" is the only way to combat that particular kind of depression, and in an appendix to that book I provided a "vocabulary of meaning" made up of phrases that support your meaning-making efforts. *Productive obsession* is a wonderful phrase to add to that vocabulary.

Productive obsession marries the idea of meaning investment — the investment we must make in our existential choices — with the idea of critical thinking. A productive obsession is an idea that you choose for good reasons and pursue with all your brain's power. It might be an idea for a novel, a business, a vaccine; it might be the solution to a personal problem. You take that seed of an idea and you bite into it, providing it with genuine neuronal devotion. A series of these productive obsessions is the exact equivalent of a lifetime of making meaning.

I've written many books on the creative process and the challenges of the creative life. These challenges include addiction (*Creative Recovery*), anxiety (*Fearless Creating*), economic survival (*Creativity for Life*), negative self-talk (*Affirmations for Artists*), and learning self-coaching skills (*Coaching the Artist Within*). I hope that *Brainstorm* will be a valuable addition to that literature. The habit of mind I describe in these pages is the best way to get your novel, screenplay, symphony, or other creative project launched and finished. Productively obsessing is the mind-set of the creative person.

Throughout this book I'll be referring to the productive obsession group that I facilitate online. I'd like to take a moment here to acknowledge the members of that group and to thank them all for participating and sharing. That group may or may not exist by the time this book gets into your hands, but if you'd like to know whether it's still operational, drop me a line at ericmaisel@hotmail.com. If it happens not to be — or if you prefer to start your own group — I have included guidelines for doing that in the appendix.

This book is a quick afternoon's read — and prepares you for a lifetime of work. If you take my suggestions and accept my challenges, you'll embark on a journey more amazing than any you could contrive by land, sea, or air. You'll activate your imagination, awaken your memory, and enlist billions of neurons in the service of your passions and ideals. There are many books on the market that help you extinguish your unwanted, unproductive obsessions. I want to impress on you that obsessing has its positive side too. This book champions and salutes that positive side and the unrivaled power of productive obsessions.

chapter one

The Logic of Brainstorms

To be the ethical, engaged, creative, successful, and lively human being you intend to be, you need your brain. But it is not enough to possess a perfectly good brain — you must also use it. If you don't use your brain you will find yourself trapped in trivialities, condemned to impulsivity, led around by anxiety, and duller and sadder than you have any need to be. The cliché is true: your mind is a terrible thing to waste.

People waste their brains. They allow themselves to worry about next to nothing, wasting neurons. They allow themselves to grow numb with distractions, wasting neurons. They allow themselves to be ruled by a perpetual to-do list, running from errand to chore to chore to errand, wasting neurons. Because they have not trained themselves to aim their brain in the direction of rich and rewarding ideas, ideas worth the wholesale enlistment of neurons, they stay mired in the mental equivalent of a rat race, spending their neuronal capital on spinning hamster wheels.

Our culture applauds this brain abdication. It needs you to care about the latest movie, the latest gadget, the latest sermon, the latest investment opportunity. Every aspect of our culture has something to sell you and needs to grab your attention. Marketers do not want you to be thinking too strenuously about your budding symphony or your scientific research and miss their sales pitch. What if you didn't answer your phone when it rang? How could they telemarket? What if you didn't check your email every few minutes? What good would their banner ads do? Your brainstorms are dollars out of their pockets.

This antipathy to rich thinking occurs at home, at school, among friends, and even with your mate. Parents tell you to clean your room, not to create your own cosmology myths. Teachers tell you to do math this hour and history the next, not to turn your brain over to a magnificent obsession. Friends ask you to shop, not to think; to play cards, not to think; to join them at a hot new restaurant, not to think; to watch a can't-miss television show, not to think. Your wife doesn't say, "Honey, let's spend a few hours thinking!" Your husband doesn't ask, "Dear, what big ideas are you working on?" Indeed, if it could be put to a vote, thinking might well be outlawed. Expect such a proposition on your ballot soon.

The good news is that you can jump off this bandwagon and opt for brainstorms. For thousand of years, our wisest philosophers have asserted that the trick to creating an authentic life is taking charge of how you use your brain. It is up to you whether you will dumb yourself down or smarten yourself up. If you opt to smarten yourself up by cultivating rich ideas with weight and worth, you will get to make meaning in ways that few people experience. The person next to you may think that the epitome of brain powering is a sharp game of bridge or a rousing afternoon with a crossword puzzle. You will discover that real brain power is holding a rich idea over time as you productively obsess your novel into existence, build your remarkable business, or aid in the understanding of some profound scientific puzzle.

You learn to opt for brainstorms, for big thinking over time, and by doing so you fulfill your promise — and your promises to yourself. An idea for a novel sparks your imagination and, because you let it, it turns into a brainstorm. An idea for an Internet business wakes you up in the middle of the night and, because you let it, it turns into a brainstorm. A scientific problem grips you and, because you let it, it turns into a brainstorm. A brainstorm is the full activation of your neuronal forces, an activation in support of an idea that you intend to cherish and elaborate, so powerful that it amounts to a productive obsession. You work on it in the mind, by thinking, and you work on it in actuality, by actually writing, by actually running for office, by actually launching your business.

Do these brainstorms come with a money-back guarantee? Yes and no. What you are not guaranteed are successful results. You might, for example, chew on a scientific puzzle for a decade and never solve it. Albert Einstein explained, "I think and think for months and years. Ninety-nine times the conclusion is false. The hundredth time I am right." Not even that hundredth time is guaranteed you. All that you are guaranteed from a life of brainstorms is the possibility of successes — which you never would have achieved if you had avoided thinking — and pride from having lived up to your expectations for yourself. And that's everything.

Thinking is destiny. The theologian Tryon Edwards put it

this way: "Thoughts lead on to purposes; purposes go forth in actions; actions form habits; habits decide character; and character fixes our destiny." As you think, so you live. If you think about nothing, it would hardly be a surprise if you complained about feeling empty and failed to rise to most occasions. If you keep your thinking as small as possible, you will probably feel and act small. If you demand that your brain produce nothing but conventional thoughts, how can you be anything but conventional? If your idea of flexing your mind is to spin fantasies, play word games, second-guess your choices, or worry endlessly, I can picture your destiny. Can't you? Isn't it crystal clear that how you use your mind determines who you are and how you lead your life?

Live up a storm. A brainstorm. Or rather, a series of brainstorms: one after another, season after season, year after year. When you engage your mind with an idea ripe enough to drip juice, large enough to fill an auditorium, fascinating enough to seduce, gripping enough to hold you enthralled, you scoot boredom out the door, make sense of your days, and live your reasons for being. In a café across town, two students may be merrily debating the meaning of life; you are making your meaning. In a skyscraper across town, two marketers may be plotting how to grab your attention; you are safe and secure, inoculated by virtue of your brainstorm. You are too busy and engrossed to notice even your own misgivings about the universe. You have bitten into something; your own chewing drowns out the world's chatter.

It is a platitude that the average brain is not used well or often enough. This truth tends to elicit a smile, a nod, and a wink. We seem happy to collude in the idea that it is fine for brains to work at only a small percentage of their capacity, just as it is fine that workers slack off as soon as the boss disappears.

You, however, may not want to take part in this antibrain conspiracy. You may see the intimate connection between brainstorms and personal meaning: that to make the meaning you intend to make, you must use more of your brain. I hope that you will vote for brainstorms. It is their light that illuminates the darkness and their fire that warms the human heart.

DR. HEADSTONE

Where will your productive obsession take you? It's possible that having the time, the mental space, or the newly embraced inclination to tap into your immediate environs will lead you to make a major contribution to your community. Take, for example, Stanley Cogan, who, according to Sarah Kershaw writing in the *New York Times*, became president of the Queens Historical Society "after a decade of digging through old graveyards in Queens, piecing together crumbling tombstones and peering at fieldstones scrawled with faded letters."

Dr. Cogan, who spent his professional life in schools, teaching and leading, decided upon his retirement to focus on unearthing the history of Queens buried along with the departed in the borough's family cemeteries. He is motivated, he says, by his desire to bring back to life "some of the borough's earliest settlers, many of whose names — and gravestones — have long been forgotten."

Over time, your commitment to pursuing your obsession and making your work public might, as it has for

Stanley Cogan, not only garner you the personal satisfaction that comes with doing work that matters but also add a new, meaningful facet to your self-identity. Maybe you'll become obsessed with orchids, typefaces, birds, insects, or the tides: these are among the productive obsessions you'll encounter as we proceed. Maybe you'll obsess symphonies into existence, or maybe you'll solve your everyday problems. What brainstorms will you create? Aren't you curious to find out?

chapter two

Putting Your Brain into Gear

I'M SUGGESTING THAT YOU CHOOSE YOUR OBSESSIONS, rather than letting them choose you, and that you move closer to your goals by learning how to productively obsess. You create worthy obsessions that you chew on, struggle with, and love, and these serial productive obsessions become the central tool you use to manifest your potential and realize your dreams.

Rather than thinking about a million things — which amounts to thinking about nothing — and maintaining only a low-level interest in and enthusiasm about life, you announce to your brain that you have a fine use for it and that you intend to move it into a higher gear. Your brain is an engine meant to perform in that higher gear and, having been waiting for your invitation, it will respond beautifully.

Most of our obsessions are not of our own choosing and do not serve us. They arise because we are anxious creatures, and our unproductive thoughts cycle repeatedly to the beat of our anxiety. Against our will, we obsess about the indignity of getting older, about changing our partner's supercilious attitude, about reconciling with a hostile parent, about catching a dreaded disease, about securing our next drink. We obsess about some trivial matter at work and, that matter having been resolved, we obsess about the next trivial matter. We obsess about things that we want to have happen, like winning the lottery, and about things that we don't want to have happen, like getting wrinkles. Our mind, which ought to be ours, gets stolen away by anxiety thieves.

Even if they do not have what's known as obsessive-compulsive disorder, many people are driven by anxiety to obsess in unproductive ways. Their unwanted, intrusive thoughts — the textbook symptom of obsession — often lead them to compulsive behaviors such as searching endlessly for youth enhancers, washing their hands raw, drinking alcoholically, or never really leaving their job at the office. Obsessive thoughts do not always lead to compulsive behaviors, but they regularly do, so regularly that the two ideas have become joined as obsessive-compulsive disorder.

These are unproductive obsessions — they do not serve us. They waste our precious time; occupy our finite neurons, robbing us of their availability; and pressure us to behave compulsively in ways that do us a great self-disservice. Anxiety fuels these obsessions, and the effort to relieve our anxiety leads us to pointless, questionable, or dangerous behaviors intended to quiet our nerves and banish the anxiety. In addition to our unproductive obsessing, our own nervous system puts us under enormous pressure and produces all sorts of unhappy effects. We become hypervigilant, easily startled, prone to opportunistic illnesses, unable to sleep, or easily fatigued. Anxiety throws us a party of problems, with unproductive obsessions the guest of honor.

This happens because of the sort of creatures we are. We have evolved with prominent bits of an ancient brain and prominent bits of a modern brain, survival instincts and a moral apparatus, primitive appetites and subtle consciousness. We are the sort of creature that can conjure worry from the look of the sky, make a choice between surviving at all costs or laying down our life for a cause, eat too many peanuts one minute and compose a haunting love song the next, and in countless curious ways contradict and confuse ourselves. Fueled by our pumping heart and our racing mind, we are pressured to obsess unproductively, or, if we can get a grip on our mind, to obsess productively.

Even though productive obsessions are rarer than unproductive ones, they indubitably exist. In clinical practice, where the word *obsession* is defined as an inappropriate, unwanted, intrusive, recurrent thought, the spotlight has naturally focused on unproductive or negative obsessions that cause pain and misery. By focusing there, mental health professionals have talked themselves out of the chance to examine the important differences between productive obsessions and unproductive ones. In short, they have defined away the possibility that some obsessions might be desirable.

In 1877 the German psychiatrist Karl Westphal defined obsession this way: "Obsessions are thoughts which come to the foreground of consciousness in spite of and contrary to the will of the patient, and which he is unable to suppress although he recognizes them as abnormal and not characteristic of himself." If only Westphal had called these particular intrusive thoughts "negative obsessions" or "unproductive obsessions," the door might have remained open for clinicians to learn about — and ultimately advocate for — productive obsessions.

Clinicians label all obsessions as negative by definition. In real life, however, people regularly experience other sorts of obsessions that not only serve them beautifully but also constitute an essential part of their effort to make personal meaning. An idea for a novel arises in them, and they begin to obsess about it. The problem of how to get libraries funded in third world countries vexes them, and they obsess about an answer. An issue like freedom consumes them, and they obsess documents like the Bill of Rights into existence.

It is fair to call these genuine obsessions rather than mere interests or even passions, because of the internal pressure generated. When a person really bites into a mental task, she generates a demand: she suddenly demands of herself that she produce this novel, invention, or symphony, that she find this vaccine or solve that riddle in higher mathematics, that she turn her idea into some appropriate reality. A demand is created that is fueled by her need to make personal meaning. This demand amounts to real pressure, as real as any pressure a human being can generate. One moment she is idly weeding the garden; the next moment an idea for a screenplay strikes and she feels compelled to drop everything and get to work.

Whether or not she would consciously put it this way, a certain calculation, culminating in a decision, has occurred in her brain. She has calculated that this screenplay matters. She has decided that this is one of the activities that will define her time on earth and that has the potential to make her feel proud of herself. It is that big a thing; and with that bigness come pressure and a real measure of discomfort. This pressure, a combination of excitement at having discovered something worth doing, turmoil as thoughts collide and ideas morph, and fear of not succeeding, can cause sleepless nights, irritability, chewed fingernails — and also great satisfaction and moments of pure bliss.

This pressure may feel unbearable at times, but it is the logical consequence of turning ourselves over to a pressing existential demand. A storm is created in the brain as meaning is sparked, passions inflamed, and anxieties stoked. It suddenly matters that we write our novel or aid in freeing a subjugated people; and when something matters, the mind engages and the body revs up. We have no choice but to live with this pressure. If the thought is of our own choosing, if it connects to our passions, interests, and existential needs, if it is our best guess as to how we should take responsibility for our freedom, then we embrace the subsequent pressure, endure it, and do our work.

Many people dream of meeting their meaning needs without having to risk a brainstorm. They hope that by "emptying their mind" or "just being" they can make sufficient meaning. They cross their fingers that they can pursue some interest with only mild energy and occasional attention and reap sufficient meaning benefits. They prefer doing "just enough" rather than taking the lead, they shut themselves down when they find themselves on the verge of a fiery pursuit, they back away from hard intellectual tasks and from projects that they fear will tax them. They know that they are not doing enough to support personal meaning — and that knowledge makes them blue — but they have decided, more or less subconsciously, that it is better to be safe than stirred up.

To do this is to lose. We want more rather than fewer brainstorms. They are the way that we make meaning and the way that civilization progresses. Scientific obsessions lead to miracle drugs, artistic obsessions lead to symphonies, humanitarian obsessions lead to freedom and justice. Productive obsessions are our lifeblood, both for the individual and for all humanity. We should not fear them simply because they put us under unwanted pressure, lend a compulsive edge to our behaviors, or in other ways discomfort and threaten us. Rather, we should learn how to encourage and manage them.

See for yourself. A productive obsession is nothing but a passionately held idea that serves your meaning-making efforts. See if the upside of making personal meaning by productively obsessing doesn't outweigh the downside of pressuring yourself. Expect to feel challenged; also expect to feel rewarded. I want you to learn firsthand what productively obsessing feels like, what can be accomplished, and what benefits this active meaning-making provides.

THE LINE BETWEEN PRODUCTIVE AND UNPRODUCTIVE

An observer might doubt that your obsession with, say, adding more lights to your Christmas display as your children go hungry or finding another bird to sketch while your mate pines away for you really amounts to a productive obsession. While it is up to you to judge and not up to others, I hope that you will bring your conscience to the table, look at the consequences and ramifications of the obsessions you choose, and make sure that they are really productive ones. Analyze your obsessions before giving yourself over to them, ensuring that they meet your criteria for goodness and soundness.

It's interesting to ponder the curious obsessions of our fellow human beings. Take, for instance, the obsession of the Snowflake Man. Housed in the Buffalo Museum of Science is a recently digitized collection of the snow crystal photography of Wilson Alwyn Bentley. Bentley, born in 1865, grew up in the Vermont countryside, where he remained his entire life, eventually becoming known as the Snowflake Man because of his unrelenting quest to freeze-frame snow crystals.

At fifteen, he was given a microscope and immediately began his lifelong love affair with capturing images of snow crystals. Daunted by the process of keeping snowflakes frozen long enough to be able to draw their "exquisite geometrical intricacies" while viewing them through his microscope, at seventeen he requested and received his first photography equipment from his parents. At nineteen, experimenting with conjoining his microscope and his bellows camera, he produced the first photomicrograph of a snow crystal. Bentley devoted his life to amassing the world's best, most complete, and most accurate collection of snow crystal photomicrographs, many of which survive today.

Bentley wrote in his notebook of 1910, "The experience of the search for new forms, the rare delight of seeing for the first time these exquisite lineaments under a microscope, the practical certainty that never again will one be found just like this one . . . is an experience so rare, so truly delightful that once undergone is never forgotten." Because Bentley fell in love with the beauty of snowflakes and because he was dedicated to sharing with the world the beauty he saw, all of us who love nature have benefitted.

chapter three

Large Neuronal Gestalts of Long Duration

W HY AM I LOBBYING FOR PRODUCTIVE OBSESSIONS? Because doing things by half produces sad human beings. Yes, the pressure to obsess can prove disturbing. But taking insufficient interest in your own thoughts is even more disturbing. It is existentially dangerous not to feel as if you are making meaning: going through life without passion and purpose provokes meaning crises. It is psychologically disturbing to look at yourself in the mirror and see a person who might have done this but didn't, who loves that but, for some odd reason, takes no interest in it. Yes, some obsessions may have a dark side. But so do boredom and passivity.

Some might argue that it is a mistake to advocate for obsessions, that obsessions are always dangerous, that they are invariably symptoms of mental distress, and that even if a given obsession is in some sense valuable, permission to productively obsess opens oneself up to unproductive obsessing, just as getting a taste for Scotch opens up a predisposed person to alcoholism. My response is: "Nobody knows," since this territory has not yet been investigated.

The medical and mental health professions have no way of knowing if all obsessions are dangerous. They have no proof that turning oneself over to productive obsessions opens up the floodgates to unproductive ones. They can't even hazard a guess. In the absence of knowledge, we are as entitled to use great art and great science as evidence for productive obsessions as they are to use clinical patients as evidence for dangerous obsessions. And they won't find it easier to provide an answer in the future, because the question is not strictly a medical or psychiatric one.

The ultimate answer is an existential one having to do with the nature of consciousness, the human condition, and the individual valuing of life. What if it turns out that to lead a life that makes an individual proud, she is obliged to engage her mind in exactly this way, in a way that "ups the ante" and permits her to focus on her existential priorities? If that turns out to be the case then she will find herself considering any side effects, such as fatigue or agitation, acceptable. It isn't that she wants the fatigue or the agitation. Because she wants to make herself proud, she decides to deal with the attendant discomfort.

Before we can answer the question of whether productive obsessing is something to shun or to value, first it would be helpful to know what consciousness is — not only in a biochemical sense but also in a way that does justice to our felt experience of individuality and instrumentality. To venture into that territory would lead us into debates about determinism and free will, daunting infinite regression arguments about ever-smaller little men (or women) sitting on the shoulders of other little men (or women), and so on. Endless competing conceptualizations of consciousness fill books too heavy to lift. All these competing conceptualizations permit us to say the following: no one knows what consciousness is. So how can we rule out the possible value of productive obsessing?

Consider one model of consciousness. Susan Greenfield, in her excellent *Journey to the Centers of the Mind*, argues for a "neuronal gestalt" theory of consciousness. In her model, what distinguishes one thought from another are the number of neurons that gather to accomplish the work of thinking and how long that "neuronal cloud" lasts. One thought is larger and lasts longer than another thought by virtue of the twin facts that more neurons have gathered to do that work and that those gathered neurons do not disperse quickly.

In his review of Greenfield's book, Anthony Campbell explains: "She provides detailed arguments in support of the view that the cortex of the brain contains groups of neurons that come together in dynamic cooperatives. These are not fixed structures but rather temporary associations that last for varying lengths of time. In a felicitous phrase she compares them to 'clouds in the brain,' coming or going as thoughts and associations move through the mind. . . . Experimental evidence exists which suggests that these fluctuating associations of neurons really do exist."

Doesn't this model suggest some fascinating possibilities with respect to obsession? What if a productive obsession is a large neuronal gestalt of long duration — a big idea that lasts a long time — and an unproductive obsession is a small neuronal gestalt with a long duration — a small, pesky idea that lasts a long time? If this were true, it would mean that the problem was not the lengthy duration of a thought but only the thought's "smallness." Our goal would be to create large neuronal gestalts of long duration.

Maybe the following is more accurate: that a productive obsession is a large neuronal gestalt of long duration arising from "fortunate reasons," and an unproductive obsession is a large neuronal gestalt of long duration arising from "unfortunate reasons." That is, obsessing may simply be the formation of large neuronal gestalts of long duration — sometimes neurons gather in the service of the person, and sometimes they gather to do some disservice. In this view, not all large neuronal gestalts of long duration would be wanted, but only the ones that arise from "fortunate reasons." If this were true, to strive to dismantle every neuronal gestalt of long duration would amount to throwing the baby out with the bathwater. Rather, we would want to pick and choose among them.

The idea of large neuronal gestalts of long duration also suggests an answer to a charge that might be leveled against productive obsessions: that what I am talking about is only "metaphoric obsession," that it is only a definitional ploy to elevate mere passion, interest, or enthusiasm to some semantically charged, enriched level and not a true and dramatic brain event. Lennard Davis articulates this complaint in his book *Obsession*:

> It may be objected that what I've just highlighted isn't obsession in a psychiatric sense, but more properly concerns an interest, a preoccupation, a fixation, or perhaps just a hobby. Indeed, in recent lectures I have given to psychotherapists, psychiatrists, and psychoanalysts, several objected that I was using the term "obsession" in a rather loose way.... [One] found himself very irritated with me, saying that I was confusing a cultural activity with a brain-induced, life-and-death

issue, and that he himself had a patient with OCD who might die within in a few weeks. How could I equate a [fascination with] perfume with this kind of real suffering?

This complaint is related to one about abuse of clinical language, such that everyone who grows antsy has adult attention deficit disorder, everyone made blue by the appearance of a cloud has clinical depression, and everyone with a drawer of rolled socks has OCD. "Productive obsession" could be charged with being an example of both clinical creep and linguistic manipulation. It is neither. Rather, it is a phrase that captures the essence of dramatic brain-based events. It is not a mere product of language; it is not a clinical term with which to mount a bandwagon. Productive obsessions are precious human phenomena that allow for masterworks, great ideas, and the application of brain potential to everyday matters.

IMPRACTICAL AND EPHEMERAL

What if large neuronal gestalts of long duration start to form in your brain around the idea of textile art? What might result if you wed your art to a commitment to preserving the environment? Maybe creations such as those of three 2009 exhibits curated by Julia Dixon for ArtsWestchester. In "Hanging by a Thread," sixteen artists collaborate "to foster a dialogue about environmental conservation and the related issues of consumerism, commodity, climate and culture."

Among the exhibiting artists is Elizabeth Morisette, an

artist who is obsessed with using everyday objects that "have a history," such as zippers, hair curlers, coupons, poker chips, and buttons, and who teaches children around the country to create art using salvaged materials. Morisette's obsession with recycling goes beyond her collectable art; she recently moved to a new home where she remodeled the bathrooms from floor to ceiling with recycled materials.

While her weavings and sculptures reveal an intense commitment to discarded object art, Morisette states that in the end she would simply "like for viewers of my work to rethink how they use and dispose of items they use every day." "Impractical" artwork of this sort, meant to comment on our culture and the human condition, comes into being because a person is obsessing in a nonclinical, high-powered way. This is not a mere hobby for the artist: it is the way she makes meaning. Large neuronal gestalts of long duration are the roiling clouds in her sky, and from them arrive showers of assemblages.

chapter four

Choosing Your
Productive Obsession

THE PRODUCTIVE OBSESSION YOU WANT TO CULTIVATE should be rooted in love, interest, and a desire to better our shared circumstances. It should be large, in the sense that it matches your desires, dreams, goals, and ambitions. Say, for example, that you produce one-of-a-kind water jars but that it's been your secret ambition to tackle a large ecological art project. If the sale of your water jars pays the rent, they probably regularly push the eco-art project right out of your mind and off the table. In this way our large projects get lost and vanish. If you wanted to try your hand at a month of productive obsessing, you might choose the eco-art project, even if making that choice involves you in the real risk that your income will dip that month.

Choose an obsession that is grand — or one that at least isn't too small. Choose an obsession that will gratify you — that genuinely connects to your interests, passions, and existential needs. Choose an obsession with some guts — one that has some weight, some meat on its bones, some heft. Choose an obsession with the potential to galvanize you — you want to be awakened, to experience your adrenaline flowing, to feel revved up and driven. Choose an obsession that amounts to a gamble. If you're too sure of the outcome, you're very likely to bore yourself.

Choose an obsession with a nameable goal built in. It is one thing to obsess about the nature of warfare and to play out mock battles in your head. It is quite another to obsess about re-creating the Battle of Gettysburg in a book, about filming a doc-umentary about a current civil war somewhere in the world, or about presenting the best available information to the students you teach. The first obsession amounts to pleasant fantasy; the other three point you in the direction of reality and accom-plishment.

Obsess about an idea and not about yourself. There is a world of difference between obsessing on "I wonder if I have it in me to raise money?" and "I wonder how to get third world libraries funded?" There is a profound difference between ob-sessing on "I wonder if I have any talent?" and "I wonder how I can translate my love of the desert into concrete images?" There is a profound difference between obsessing about your-self and obsessing about the thing you want to tackle. The first is an unproductive obsession; the second is a productive one.

Choose an obsession that you can really gnaw on. You want to feel involved, tested, and stretched. Maybe you think that you would like to "do a little writing," while at the same time you harbor the secret wish of writing a full-scale biogra-phy of Emma Darwin, someone you find as fascinating as her famous husband. Choose Emma over "a little writing." Choose an idea that is as large and as great as you are. Even if you do not feel large and great, try to ignore your doubts and dispute your negative self-talk and choose Emma or her equivalent. Choosing "a little writing" will tire you out as soon as you choose it. Choosing Emma may scare you — but once the fright subsides, you will have a delicious idea to sink your teeth into.

Choose an obsession that is ethical, that meets your moral standards. You may have no real way of knowing if the novel you intend to write or the business you intend to start will prove to be an ethical plus or minus: is obsessing a laser into existence a good thing or a bad thing, given that it can be used both by armies and by doctors? Still, try to intuit if your obsession is likely to amount to a moral plus or minus; and if it is long on interest but short on values, skip it. Why violate your principles for the sake of maintaining your interest when there are other, worthier obsessions to pursue?

Choose an obsession congruent with your current self. People often possess ideas they've harbored for a long time either that they've pursued to some extent already — the quarter-written novel, the half-finished degree in architecture — or that they have long imagined pursuing but have never gotten around to starting. Sometimes those ideas are still the right, rich, and true ideas to pursue — and sometimes they are relics that have little or no present value. Before you choose an idea from the past as your productive obsession, make sure that you are genuinely passionate about it and that it is relevant to your current meaning needs.

Choose an obsession that taps into your natural genius, talents, and abilities. Do you have a green thumb but have never allowed yourself to obsess gardens into existence? Are you a frustrated math whiz who could do the math associated with cosmology if you set your mind to it? Are you a splendid planner who could organize something as large as a D-day invasion, if only you found the right project? If you have a choice between two equally attractive productive obsessions, why not choose the one that allows you to make use of your gifts?

Let's put all the above into a sentence with a lot of "g" words: Choose a grand, good, goal-oriented, growth-inspiring, gratifying, grown-up, gutsy productive obsession that allows you to make use of your natural genius and your gifts, that provides you with something to really grapple with and gnaw on, and that is more a gamble than it is guaranteed.

What merits productive obsessing? The answer must be: it's your call. But do take the above criteria into consideration. You may be in the habit of scaring yourself out of tackling large ideas, avoiding the heavy lifting that comes with ambitious projects, and blending into the background. If these are your habits, you may incline toward choosing as a productive obsession something too puny and uninteresting. Try not to talk yourself out of the biggest productive obsession possible. If you've bitten off more than you can chew, you can let it go later — that may disappoint you, but it won't disgrace you. Wouldn't you rather attempt your equivalent to *War and Peace* than settle for some additional blog entries? Maybe you won't succeed — but maybe you will. Set the bar high on your productive obsession.

Choose your productive obsession right now. Maybe you know exactly which one to select. Even if you're positive, give your idea a once-over and make sure it meets your current meaning needs and intentions. Maybe you have several good candidates but aren't sure which one to choose. Take your best guess, and commit to obsessing for a month. Maybe none of the ideas you've examined seems worthy, grand, or interesting enough. Then stop everything, get as quiet as you can, and invite the right idea in. If you are open to it, it will come.

When you've settled on your productive obsession, jot it down. Your choice might sound like "writing that novel about my grandmother," "bringing my art therapy practice to orphanages in Africa," "understanding evolution so well that I can write about it intelligently," "getting my products in stores nationwide," "recording my first album," or "saving that wilderness area just north of town from development." Maybe yours will sound less ambitious than these; maybe yours will sound more ambitious. Maybe yours will involve you in dynamic collaborations; maybe yours will have a go-it-alone feel to it. Whatever its particulars, make it *yours*. Get it named — and get ready to let it invade you.

DECONSTRUCTING "GRAND"

I've suggested that your productive obsession be as grand as you can make it. However, productive obsessions serve many useful purposes, from channeling passion to binding existential anxiety and helping us feel calmer, so if pursuing a "modest" or "small" passion with obsessive intensity serves your emotional and existential needs, then by all means pursue it. I would only ask you to go through the process of mindfully choosing, to make sure you are not passing up some grand passion that you would actually love to pursue.

The artist Jacob Marrel's willingness to include his

stepdaughter, Maria Sibylla Merian, in the lessons he gave his pupils in Frankfurt in the 1650s produced a passion in her for drawing the natural world and led her to record some of life's heretofore unseen processes. Born in 1647, Merian pursued an unconventional life in which her work as an artist, entomologist, and botanist took precedence over her comfort and even her health. She risked everything, at the age of fifty-two, to travel with her daughter Dorothea to Suriname to study specimens of indigenous plants and animals — which she had only seen dried in collections — alive in their natural South American habitat.

As Merian's biographer, Kim Todd, writes: "Her careful observations of iridescent blue morpho butterflies and giant flying cockroaches made her one of the first to describe metamorphosis . . . and laid the groundwork for modern-day biological science, particularly ecology." Merian died in 1717, having led a life of "untiring observation," an almost unparalleled "example of single-minded scientific obsession." Did her desire to see living things alive in nature, rather than dried and mounted in museums, amount to a modest and small obsession or an immodest and grand one? Who knows where your "small" obsessions may lead?

chapter five

Making the Ordinary
Extraordinary

I'VE SUGGESTED THAT YOUR PRODUCTIVE OBSESSION should be a grand and mighty thing, a place of genuine interest and existential utility, because I want you to set the bar high and make yourself proud. But you can also use this process to deal with any problem or concern that confronts you. Productive obsessing is a way of using your mind that you can apply equally to the ordinary challenges of life and to extraordinary ideas that bubble up. The process is one of training your neurons to gather in the service of some intellectual task and to stay gathered over time. That task might be birthing a novel, but it could just as well be analyzing your career choices or your health-care options.

Maybe your most pressing concern right now is finding your mother a bed in an assisted-living facility. Maybe it's making arrangements to keep your business running while you recuperate from an operation. Maybe it's making sense of your impending retirement. Maybe it's figuring out how to fight a battle that's looming at work. It is altogether legitimate to productively obsess about such ordinary matters. You can productively obsess to tackle any pressing concern, whether it be grand or mundane, exotic or everyday. It would be nice to use your brain in the service of your beautiful dreams, but there is no reason to reserve it for only such purposes.

Sometimes the object of your productive obsession may be the novel you intend to write, the business you want to build, or the medical research you hope to undertake. At other times the object will be an everyday problem you need to solve, such as how to organize your living space or whether to look for a new job. You set the bar exactly where it needs to be set, sometimes nearer the sky, sometimes more at eye level.

Andy, a lawyer, chose as his productive obsession the ordinary matter of finding his contract work less boring. He'd set up his life in a manner that he thought was well-nigh ideal, staying at home with his young children while his wife worked in the world, and making enough money from his home-based legal contract work to be a real contributor to the family's finances. His contract work paid well and could be contained to two or three hours a day. What setup could be better? Yet something had gone wrong: Andy's contract work bored him so much that he could hardly turn to it, and he found himself growing more depressed with each passing week.

He joined the cyberspace productive obsession group that I run, with the intention of dreaming a large nonprofit into existence, something that would feed his interests in a way that his legal contract work could not. But after two weeks of trying to maintain that obsession he realized that he'd put the cart before the horse: the legal contract work was piling up, making him miserable, and it made no sense to try to turn his brain over to a beautiful pie-in-the-sky project when this pressing work required his immediate attention. So he lowered the bar to eye level. What was going on? Why had the contract work become so odious?

He realized that he didn't want to turn this attempt at analysis into an unproductive obsession that amounted to little more than worrying about the situation. He wanted to wonder deeply about it, not worry about it, and he sensed the thinness of the line between wonder and worry. He made a deal with himself that if the effort began to feel like a mistake — if it began to feel like a charming opportunity to unproductively obsess — he'd stop and splash some cold water on his face. At the same time, he understood that spending a few hours in the territory of worry was necessary and ultimately fruitful.

On the first day he discovered that his contract work felt more approachable. Something about deciding to productively obsess a solution into existence instantly changed his relationship to his work. It was as if a breath of optimism had entered that dark home office where his contract work lived. He couldn't quite do the work yet, but he did open the door to the office, raise the blinds, open the window, and let the spring breeze blow through. He even did a bit of organizing — not more than ten minutes' worth, but ten minutes more than he'd done in weeks.

This quick result surprised him. He hadn't yet done any thinking on his problem, but simply declaring that he would do that thinking seemed to make a difference and create an opening. Why, he wondered, should merely declaring that he was about to productively obsess about his contract work sufficiently change his attitude that he could enter his office and raise the blinds? He nursed that idea, pursued it, made some notes, and by the third day was knocking out his contract work — even without an answer to his question.

He continued to obsess on the matter. What was going on? What had changed such that on Monday he couldn't approach his contract work and by Thursday he was knocking it out? He concluded that he had built up the work into a kind of monster, internally bad-mouthing it as the most boring, unworthy work a human being could ever undertake. By choosing to productively obsess about his horror of tackling the contract work, he'd begun to examine his assumptions and listen to his negative self-talk with a new ear — and that proved enough. He used his brain's full power to test his assumptions and examine his self-talk and concluded — at first subconsciously and then consciously — that his contract work was simply not that bad.

For years he'd been too distracted — by parenting, by running a household, by all the everyday chores that distract people — to fight off his growing unhappiness with his contract work. Because he did not possess the mental space to fight it off, that unhappiness had festered and grown. The instant Andy chose to examine the matter, he produced the mental space to reconsider whether the contract work was all that bad — and he discovered that it wasn't. Within weeks of that discovery he was able to move on to the productive obsession he had hoped to entertain in the first place, dreaming that nonprofit into existence.

The challenges you face are the exact ones you need to tackle. They may prove hard to tackle for exactly the same reason that Andy's problem with his contract work had grown intractable: if you don't apply your brain's full power to the matter, you don't give yourself the chance to think it through. You remain stuck in a rut, thinking the same thoughts today that you thought yesterday, locked into a mental holding pattern in which your thoughts swirl and never land properly. When, by contrast, you announce that you intend to productively obsess about the challenge at hand, your brain is alerted to the fact that you intend to operate differently. Your neurons stand at attention, and thinking commences.

By productively obsessing about ordinary matters, you provide yourself with the extraordinary opportunity to bring optimism, a breath of fresh air, and all your brain's power to bear on your everyday problems and challenges. Productively obsessing is the way — perhaps the only way — to birth symphonies, businesses, and medicines. But side by side with your desire to birth symphonies, businesses, or medicines is your need to meet your everyday challenges of mood, personality, and circumstance. Use your brain there too.

SHARED OBSESSIONS

Productive obsessions come in a vast number of flavors limited only by the interests of human beings and the ways in which they find personal meaning. Many of these are shared obsessions: an author becomes obsessed with a subject, and subsequently readers become obsessed with the author's vision (think of the fans of James Joyce or Jane Austen); countless visual artists share an obsession with the power and possibility of abstraction; an untold number of medical researchers are obsessed with unlocking the mysteries of the human genome. Then there are the fans of robotics.

Consider Ian Bernstein, creator of a website filled with links to and information about BEAM robotics, the special area of robotics focused on scavenging parts, recycling components, and employing solar energy. Obsessed as a little kid with taking apart things such as cameras and radios, as an adolescent Bernstein competed in a number of robotics competitions, including the 1998 International BEAM Robotics Games in India.

Mark Tilden, the creator of BEAM robotics, also became interested in the field at a young age. He explains, "I built my first robot doll out of wood scraps at the age of three and progressed from there to a Meccano suit of armor for the family cat at the age of six. I've been building devices ever since." A recent project? The release into the New Mexico White Sands Missile Range of the largest contiguous robot colony ever: a thousand units, each twelve inches long, three inches high, and moving about at twenty centimeters a second. "And," Tilden says with a laugh, "we might not get all of them back."

As likely as not, you are not alone in your productive obsession. There may not be an Olympics for your obsession, as there is for fans of robotics — unless, of course, you start one!

chapter six

Productive = Work

$\mathbf{I}$S A PRODUCTIVE OBSESSION really a productive obsession if you have to work at it? Isn't there some implication in the phrase that you love your productive obsession so much and are so passionate about it that it never feels like work, that it is never daunting, and that you are always smiling because you're getting to bite into something delicious? Marti, a member of my productive obsession group, expressed this wonder in the following way:

> Yesterday I went to a trunk show at a local jewelry store. I had never heard of this jewelry designer but at the store saw the photograph of her jewelry as featured in one of the major style magazines. As I looked at her creations, which were indeed beautiful, we talked. I asked her how she got into doing this. She gave the answer that often comes from people who are highly successful at a young age: she said, "Making

jewelry has been my passion since I was a little girl. I love making jewelry. I can stay up doing it until midnight and I don't notice the time going by because I love what I'm doing."

For me, writing is an obsession, but I don't always love to do it. Therein lies the problem. It's an obsession, but it's not as pure as this jewelry maker's passion appears to be. In fact, I'm not sure why writing is my obsession at all, considering that I don't always love to do it, the way she loves to create jewelry. I think the ultimate question is: if one has to work at something being a productive obsession, is it really an obsession at all?

Can you be passionate about something, obsessed with it, and still have to work hard at it? Yes! The proof that something is a legitimate productive obsession is not that it comes easily. A novelist may have one book come easily and the next book prove more challenging. That doesn't mean that she is less obsessed with the second book. It means only that the second book is harder. In fact, she may be more obsessed with the second book and may be traveling with it to a deeper place where the answers are rich but obscured in darkness. It would be a grave mistake to suppose that the proof that you are productively obsessing is that you are finding the going easy. Much of the time it may be hard work — maybe even all the time.

Nor is there reason to suppose that you have to love what you have undertaken. You may not love turning your brain over to the question of how to get the best care for your disabled father, how to deal with the underhanded tactics of your political opponent, or how to get funding for your documentary film. You might prefer to turn your brain over to some other interest where love and passion reside. But love and passion are not the criteria; good reasons are. A productive obsession is an idea that you have good reasons for pursuing. It is the way you use your brain to handle the business of life, do the next right thing, make meaning, and make yourself proud. If genuine love, passion, and interest are fueling the idea, consider them bonuses or blessings. The point of a productive obsession is that it is productive, which translates as "I have good reasons for using my brain this way" and not "I love everything about this idea!"

Productively obsessing is a way to use your mind. It does not require that you love, honor, or cherish the object of your obsession: all that is required is that you have reasons for obsessing. Maybe you love to paint, and your new idea for a series of paintings turns into a productive obsession. That productive obsession is indeed fueled by passion and love. But maybe you also need to think through whether or not to leave your current job, a decision of considerable importance in your life. Thinking about that is likely to make you extremely anxious — still, you have good reasons to stick with that obsession, even though passion isn't fueling it and even though thinking about it makes you anxious.

Even if you do love your idea, even if it is the fruit of passion and genuine interest, you are not productively obsessing until you do the work that your idea demands. Many people are obsessed with some "big idea," but not in a productive way. They may be obsessed with creating a business that genuinely makes use of their talents or engaging in research that feels more interesting than their current niche research. But if their obsession takes them no further than wringing their hands and spinning their wheels, it is not productive. Their obsession, as excellent as it might be if they genuinely embraced it, is as negative as any other unproductive obsession while it remains a fantasy shrouded in worry.

That your idea is good does not mean that your obsession

with it is good. Being obsessed with a brilliant idea for a film for forty years and never making an effort to turn that idea into an actual film is not a productive obsession, no matter how brilliant the idea is. It is exactly the opposite: it is an unproductive obsession fueled by anxiety, kept alive by anxiety, and used to quell anxiety. It is fantasy used as defense. While you are defending yourself with your beautiful fantasy of one day making this beautiful movie, your brain is held captive and prevented from productively obsessing. Your beautiful fantasy uses up your neurons, and your life feels smaller and bleaker with those neurons tied up and unavailable.

Do the work. Productively obsessing is a way to address life, not a way to justify staying stuck in your head. It is the way you use your brain to meet your needs, whether emotional, practical, intellectual, or existential, and not a destination in itself. Imagine that your beautiful ideas are like a bountiful harvest. That harvest will rot if the food doesn't make it to the table. To get that food from the field to the table requires work, hard, slogging work. It takes real work to get that bushel of gorgeous heirloom tomatoes to market. Just looking at them is not enough: work must follow.

Consider Van Gogh. At the start of his painting career, after he'd been fired from the ministry, he envisioned paintings that he knew he couldn't yet produce. They existed in his brain, but he wasn't proficient enough to render them on canvas. He could have imagined those beautiful images, complained bitterly that they were doomed to remain mental images only, and thrown in the towel. Instead he chose a different route, the route of work. For months on end he practiced making the kinds of strokes that would enable him to paint what he saw in his mind. A cypress required this set of strokes; a fern, this set; a poplar, this set; irises, this set. He practiced and remained productive. When he felt that his repertoire of strokes was ready, he began painting. We know the results.

To pave the way for you to become as productive as Van Gogh, you'll need to let go of certain insidious notions about productive obsessions. All the following are myths worth busting:

MYTH: A productive obsession must be fueled by passion and love.

REALITY: Love and passion are splendid, but what actually fuel a productive obsession are your good reasons for pursuing it.

MYTH: The proof that a productive obsession is worth pursuing is that it feels easy.

REALITY: Thinking is not easy, and doing is not easy. Together, they don't get any easier.

MYTH: If a productive obsession isn't fun, it's not worth bothering with.

REALITY: Our life purposes include joy, but they also include a variety of other values. "Fun" is not the only value to honor and revere.

MYTH: You are working on your idea even if you are only thinking about it.

REALITY: Ideas require elaboration in order for them to grow. Only rarely can that elaboration be done entirely in the mind; as a rule it must be done at the computer, at the piano, at the easel, in the trenches.

MYTH: The only difference between a productive obsession and an unproductive one is that one is positive and the other is negative.

REALITY: Unproductive obsessions represent the misuse of your mind, the habitual giving away of neurons, and a resultant small existence. Productive obsessions represent your willingness to use your mind in the service of authentic action. This goes far beyond the simple designations of "positive" and "negative."

AN UNDERSTANDING OF WORK

Consider the case of architect William Highet, who took it upon himself to paint in true-to-life detail one section of Edinburgh's Royal Mile, the city's old-town thoroughfare.

Highet, a retired architect who practiced in Inverness, Scotland, for more than twenty years, accepted his self-created challenge in 2000 to record in scrupulous detail the most historically eclectic section of Edinburgh's Royal Mile. Before he started sketching, Highet spent long days pacing off the building frontages and many quiet Sunday mornings with his wife, Anne, precisely measuring the building frontages using a steel measuring tape. His obsession required innumerable visits to Edinburgh to catch the buildings' hues at various times of day, and after more than two years of painstaking work — re-creating every window detail, every historical feature, and every nuance of color — Highet completed his project, a painting consisting of six panels and measuring thirty feet long.

Highet's hope — that his rendering of his chosen section of the Royal Mile would be preserved — was fulfilled when the Royal Commission on the Ancient and Historical Monuments of Scotland agreed to archive his work.

Even so, when asked in an interview with Jenny Shields whether he would extend his project to additional sections of the Royal Mile, Highet responded, "I'm not ruling it out, but let's just say that at the moment I would take an awful lot of persuading."

His response was natural enough, considering that a productive obsession typically leads to exactly this amount of work. When your next productive obsession pops into your head, you will have the memory of hard work to contend with. The more we do, the more we understand what doing means, and this knowledge is bound to inform each of our subsequent decisions.

chapter seven

Are You Conflicted?

Many people are in serious conflict about whether or not they really want to accomplish much. Contemporary life aims them in the direction of accomplishment: they are supposed to choose a profession such as doctor, lawyer, accountant, engineer, entrepreneur, banker, writer, or teacher and then make their mark. They have never been told, "Become a lawyer and then do poorly." Nevertheless, they may receive direct and indirect messages from their parents, teachers, friends, and colleagues that they don't really have what it takes to succeed. Or they may come to that conclusion themselves, reframing their conclusion as "I don't like competing" or "I don't want to put in all those hours."

These conflicting messages, that you ought to succeed and that you don't have what it takes to succeed, lead to what we see so often nowadays: folks moving from one field to the next, from one degree to the next, from one job to the next, from one dream to the next, from one ambition to the next. They fail to complete things; or they complete them in a slipshod way; or they complete them by virtue of tackling only what they find easy to do. They are vaguely aware of the fact that some inner conflict is slowing them down but not aware of the extent to which the conflict is actually derailing them.

Such conflicts — between wanting to write and not feeling imaginative enough to write, between wanting to research some scientific problem but not feeling smart enough — are exacerbated by the fact that we don't love certain parts our work. We may love writing but not rewriting or selling. We may love getting an innocent defendant off but not helping the guilty ones escape justice. We may love our environmental cause but not the endless fund-raising. We may love designing interesting homes but not designing all the bread-and-butter ones. What if we love only about 8 percent or 13 percent of our work? Then we begin to fantasize about working in other fields wherein we imagine that percentage would be higher.

These conflicts — about whether we really intend to accomplish anything, whether we really love our own interests, and so on — make productive obsessing that much more difficult. First of all, neurons are being stolen in the debate. A conflict is a brain-based battle requiring the participation of neurons, leaving fewer available for large thinking. Second, the conflicts serve to burst the bubble of any large neuronal gestalts that manage to form. Some small damaging thought comes along and punctures the beautiful incipient large thought that is trying to gain a foothold. A new productive obsession is only as strong as a soap bubble and, with all those arrows of conflict flying about, one is bound to find the mark and puncture the obsession.

How can you resolve such deep-seated, intractable conflicts? The first step is to acknowledge their reality. The most difficult conflicts are those that remain out of conscious awareness. If your way of dealing with uncertainty about whether you really want to play the violin in a symphony orchestra is to sabotage auditions and generate wrist injuries rather than airing the issue, then you end up with ruined auditions, hurt wrists, and precious little insight. Because it feels so dangerous to air the conflict — what if what you learn indicts your parents or propels you out of music altogether? — you keep silent on the matter and deal with the symptoms and not with the source of the symptoms. Airing the conflict must be braved, even though the consequences may be startling, or else you will always be dealing with symptoms.

Acknowledging the reality of these inner conflicts is step one. Step two is engaging in conscious conflict resolution. You name your wishes and your fears, you defuse the fears that ought to be defused and respect those that must be honored, you come to conclusions, and you commit to your decision. This might sound like, "I need to face why I sabotage myself at auditions. What am I afraid of? Well, I think it's two major things. First, I'm afraid that I'm performing only because my parents wanted me to perform. Second, I'm afraid that I don't love classical music enough to spend a lifetime trying to master it. I think I could deal with the first fear — if it weren't for the second. I must decide if I want to spend my life playing classical music — if the answer is yes, then I have new commitments to make; if the answer is no, then I have to figure out what to do with myself."

Jennifer, a member of my productive obsession group, reported, "My department head offered me a project much larger than anything I'd ever tackled before. He wanted to give me the whole advertising budget for our department to spend any way I liked on the new media and social networking sites. I'd have to research everything, learn the language, make decisions, track outcomes, and make reports. I could feel an obsession with learning how to do this bubble up instantly, and I had no doubt that I wanted to jump right in. Then I started getting headaches and getting sick in other ways, and I could tell that I was internally fighting with myself about this challenge. I wanted to do it — but I guess it also scared me. Finally I had a frank conversation with myself about whether or not my fears were actually justified. I aired the matter as best I could and came down on my own side — and the headaches went away. Now I'm obsessing about how to spend a million dollars a month of company money — and having a great time!"

Jack explained, "My family was not highly educated, and the process of getting my doctorate in biology has put me in a funny conflict with my roots. To compensate for my fear that I don't really deserve to be a professor and that I'm a stupid person masquerading as a smart one, I've prevented myself from doing what I would really love to do, namely write a popular book about biology. I know that I could obsess about that book in a way that I can't obsess about what I currently do in my lab. But I'm prevented from starting on a popular book because 'real academics' don't do such things. If I can't work this out I'll be stuck spending my whole academic career running small experiments rather than obsessing about the big biological ideas that are really so fascinating."

Margaret reported, "I got two entirely different messages growing up. My father told me that I was brilliant and that I could do anything I wanted. My mother told me that I was incompetent and was bound to fail at everything I tried. I remember one incident vividly. I thought I'd surprise my mother by baking a cake. When she got home she yelled at me about using the wrong pan, about making a mess, about everything. To this day I'm inclined to presume that, whatever I tackle, I'm going to get it wrong. I'm also burdened by my father's message, because if I'm that gifted, then I'm miserably failing myself and everyone else by getting so little accomplished. I know that these simmering conflicts have wreaked havoc my whole life, making me slower than I really am, more fearful than I really am, and dumber than I really am. I must get them aired and resolved and come down on my own side — the clock is ticking."

Your own brain will prevent excellent brainstorms if you are conflicted about wanting those brainstorms. Are you betting too many of your chips on failure? A productive obsession is not just a neuronal event; it is also a psychological one that flows from your determination to love something, learn something, do something, and mean something. Many people are riddled with the kinds of internal conflicts that prevent them from wholeheartedly engaging with ideas. If you are one of these many, air your conflicts and resolve them.

LEVELING THE PLAYING FIELD

Freud argued that external challenges alone do not produce what he called neurosis. Some powerful internal component such as a simmering conflict is also necessary. He explained, as quoted by Robert Dilts in his article

"Resolving Conflicts with NLP": "In order to become pathogenic, external frustration must be supplemented by internal frustration." Typically this internal conflict is between a wish, for instance, that you want to write a novel, and a worry, say, that you don't have sufficient talent. This wish-and-worry dynamic plagues countless people. Or the conflict may be between a personal value, say, that you want to speak in your own voice, and a cultural value, maybe that you are supposed to blend in and bow to the common will. Inner conflicts come in countless variations.

In Freud's view, neurosis arises primarily because of these unresolved internal conflicts. He wrote, "One side of the personality stands for certain wishes, while another part struggles against them and fends them off. There is no neurosis without such a conflict." He argued that the sufferer is typically aware of only half the conflict, the wish part (the "I want to write my novel" part), and not the worry part (not the "I probably don't have enough talent" part). Or both parts may remain out of conscious awareness: the patient may not quite recognize that he is dying to speak in his own voice and may also not recognize to what extent his culture is stifling him. Because the conflict remains unconscious, the sufferer is prevented from resolving it.

Freud considered it the therapist's job to bring these conflicts out into the open. He wrote, "An effective decision can be reached only when [the two forces involved in the inner conflict] confront each other on the same ground. . . . To accomplish this is the sole task of the treatment." The psychoanalyst, through nondirective means and through techniques such as free association, helps the patient air the conflict, quite possibly for the first time ever, and find relief in that airing. But the airing is not enough. The patient gains important insight by virtue of having the conflict aired; but then he must work to actually resolve the conflict.

Naming both sides of the conflict and exposing the conflict to the light of day, thus reducing its power, is the necessary first step in eliminating it. Suddenly you know that there is a conflict and what the conflict is about. Then you endeavor to bring the conflict to some satisfactory resolution. For example, you meet your own objections by asserting that you do have the requisite talent to write your novel or the requisite courage to speak in your own voice. Having met your own objections, you are now in a position to incubate and nurture productive obsessions.

If you are harboring some powerful inner conflict, the playing field is not level. It is inclined in the directions of safety and denial. To be able to take the risks that come with productively obsessing, you must do the work of airing and resolving any simmering inner conflicts. Although they are off in a corner of your awareness, they make their presence felt in your self-talk. By closely monitoring your self-talk, you can learn which conflicts are tilting the playing field and then proceed to resolve them.

chapter eight

One Month of
Productive Obsessing

I SUGGEST TO FOLKS who want to cultivate productive obsessions that they try their hand at productively obsessing for a month. As shorthand, let's call this "the productive obsession program," though there is hardly anything programmatic about it. If there are steps to it, they are only the two most obvious ones: you choose your productive obsession, and you bite into it. The rest, as they say, is commentary, which this book provides.

A month is an interesting amount of time. Georges Simenon routinely wrote his novels in a month's time — in three weeks, actually, with a week left over for golf. In a month you could create a business plan and begin to enact it, write enough songs for an album, or track an idea from its first glow to its polished articulation. If you can get from San Francisco to Paris in twelve hours, what can't you do in a month? You could get in a lot of productive obsessing — or learn about your idiosyncratic ways of preventing yourself from using your brainpower. In a month you could produce a brainstorm or learn why you refuse to cultivate one.

Your month may fly by without your ever really getting started. That is information and probably means that most of your months fly by without your attending to your goals and dreams. Probably your ideas stay vague and swirly rather than growing ever sharper. Probably you find yourself still fighting old emotional battles. Probably the microscopic is overwhelming the grand. If your month flies by and little productive obsessing has occurred, take that as a clarion call to work your second month differently.

What are you really doing when you devote yourself to a month of productive obsessing? You are learning how to extinguish distractions so that you can concentrate; you are accepting the hard existential fact that if you intend to matter, you must act as if you matter; you are retraining your brain and asking it to stop its pursuit of fluff and worry and to embrace its own potential. In addition, you are announcing that you prefer grand pursuits to ordinary ones; you are standing in solidarity with other members of your species who have opted for big thinking and big doing; and you are turning yourself over, even to the point of threat and exhaustion, to your own loves and interests.

A brainstorm is a brain event orchestrated by a human being. It is not a brain event in a bell jar or a brain event separated from the facts of your existence. It is not a mechanical firing of neurons. It is a human thing created by a human being as part of that human being's life plan. It is a symphony wanting to exist in the heart of a composer. It is a theory of evolution not yet formulated in the heart of a naturalist. It is a nonprofit arising from a flesh-and-blood person's actual compassion. Your monthlong program, which becomes an infinitely long program as you repeat it, is a program not for brains in bell jars but for individuals who want to assert their individuality and manifest their values.

Cultivating productive obsessions has little to do with egotism. Ego requires few neurons; any idiot can be an egotist. There are no greater narcissists than ordinary people who think about nothing and from that throne of vacuity make grandiose pronouncements. My hunch is that you'll experience your month of productive obsessing not as ego driven but rather as a month of pure service: service to an admirable idea of your choosing. We get smaller when we are not productively obsessing: by not engaging our brain, we waste our neurons on preening and posturing.

This is an action-oriented program. You take a mental vacation from your everyday way of being, from your affinity groups, your Twittering, your social networking, your Internet surfing, your blog reading, your worries and doubts, your constant neuronal firing in the service of not all that much, and you turn an idea that fascinates you into something real in the world: a substantial chunk of your novel, a robust business plan, a round of excellent experiments, something that requires both thinking and elbow grease. This productive obsession program is not about spending time in the brain as if the brain were a destination. It is about using your brain in the service of the work you intend to accomplish.

What should you expect to accomplish in a month? Not everything, but something real. You should expect to feel yourself move from wish-and-worry to thoughtful action. You should move beyond trying to choose a worthy obsession to choosing one and committing to it. You should experience the felt sense that there is something beautiful and magical about attending to real work. Will you get to the top of your mountain in a month's time? Probably not. But it is excellent to have a mountaintop as a goal and to expect to rise to such heights.

Let's say that you love to hike in the mountains but rarely go hiking. You start the productive obsession program and set as your grand goal climbing a famous peak. It wouldn't surprise anyone, yourself included, if you failed to achieve your lofty goal in a single month, given that you haven't been hiking for years. But what if setting the goal at that lofty height provided exactly the spark to get you hiking again? Is it a success or a failure if you do not make it to the top of Mount Everest by the end of the month but you do go hiking three times a week in your own neighborhood — three weekly hikes more than you were enjoying before you began the program? How can that not be considered a success?

You do not need to clear your calendar in order to begin — you couldn't clear your calendar if you wanted to. You do not need to quit your day job, wait for your nine-year-old to begin college, or get the buy-in from your busy mate. You do not need to clean cobwebs out of the basement corners or buy a productive obsession outfit. There are some things that you'll want to do, and I will describe them in a subsequent chapter. But in essence there is nothing to do but to begin. Your brain is waiting, and it is the only tool necessary.

Should you start on the first of the month? Should you skip this month, since it includes your two-week vacation to London? Should you wait until June, when you stop teaching? Be sensible, be reasonable, but also be adamant. If it feels right to start on the first of the month rather than midmonth, then wait until the first; but when the first arrives and you begin to waver, do not accept your sudden intuition that you ought to start on the second. If it is sensible to skip this month, then skip it; but begin on the first of next month. Be sensible, be reasonable, but err on the side of *starting*.

Begin to look forward to your coming brainstorm. Begin to smile at the thought of it. Began to organize a bit in anticipation of clearing the decks. Begin to wean yourself from this or that distracting activity. Get ready. Soon you will begin a fine month of productive obsessing. I hope you are eager!

ENDURANCE

Real work that we do in the service of our goals and dreams requires endurance. Our work may bring us joy and deep satisfaction, but on many days it will also bring us headaches, doubts, and difficulties. We must demand of ourselves that we endure all that. Maintaining meaning is not a variety of fun; it is work, the work that an existentially aware individual engages in as she manifests her principles, acts as a moral instrument, and makes use of her brain cells. Hard work of this sort requires our staying power.

You may think that your day job, your chores, and your responsibilities are the work of your life and that your productive obsession should be the place where you get to play. Not true. Your productive obsession is the place where you birth song cycles, cure diseases, build businesses, and solve personal and intellectual problems. Some wonderful play is involved, but in essence it is serious work. Get ready for it by preparing to endure. Make a conscious decision not to give up. Little good comes from giving up.

Below are some endurance quotations. Commit to your productive obsession by choosing one as your quote of the month, displaying it prominently, and learning it by heart. Adopt it as your motto. If necessary, shorten it or personalize it. Or, if none of these quotations resonates for you, find or create your own.

Eleven Endurance Quotations

1. "I know quite certainly that I myself have no special talent; curiosity, obsession and dogged endurance, combined with self-criticism, have brought me to my ideas." — ALBERT EINSTEIN

2. "Endurance is the first lesson a child should learn because it's the one they will most need to know." — JEAN JACQUES ROUSSEAU

3. "Endurance is patience concentrated." — THOMAS CARLYLE

4. "Endurance is one of the most difficult disciplines, but it is to the one who endures that the final victory comes." — BUDDHA

5. "As a camel beareth labor, and heat, and hunger, and thirst, through deserts of sand, and fainteth not; so

the fortitude of a man shall sustain him through all perils." — AKHENATON

6. "Beyond talent lie all the usual words: discipline, love, luck — but most of all, endurance." — JAMES BALDWIN

7. "It is within the process of endurance that opportunity reveals itself." — CHIN-NING CHU

8. "I never was content unless I was trying my skill or testing my endurance." — JIM THORPE

9. "Endurance pierces marble." — MOROCCAN PROVERB

10. "Heroism is endurance for one moment more." — GEORGE F. KENNAN

11. "Enjoy what you can, endure what you must." — GOETHE

Pick your favorite endurance quote — and use it!

chapter nine

Creativity and Productive Obsessions

W HAT PROCESS DO PEOPLE GO THROUGH as they attempt to arrive at their productive obsession? As a creativity coach I work with creative and performing artists, and as a meaning coach I work with individuals looking for help with their meaning challenges. In this chapter, let me share with you how the first group chooses and frames their productive obsessions. In the next chapter we'll explore how meaning clients choose and frame theirs.

Stephanie explained, "I have been writing or storytelling my whole life, and I have always wanted to make a living as a writer. But I always let things hold me back. I let having a day job sidetrack me; I let fear sidetrack me. I procrastinate wildly; and yet the less I write, the unhappier I become with everything. I can't let go of the desire to write, but I need to let go of the unproductive obsessing I do about writing — the worry about not being good enough, the worry that I won't be able to make a living, the worry that I won't be able to think of anything wonderful to write about. I get more and more stressed out, and I write less and less, and it becomes a particularly nasty downward spiral. Now it's time to break out of the negative cycle and build a positive one, even if pushing past my worries is scary. I have good stories to tell, and I'll have things to teach people about their own creativity and breaking blocks once I break through mine. My productive obsession: to plan and complete a novel and get it ready to submit to agents."

Belle wrote, "I normally draw in my studio two to three hours a day, Monday through Thursday. Basically this is 'scheduled creativity,' and it works for me — up to a point. Any other time I think about my artwork, which is many times a day every day of the week, I might make a note to myself so I don't forget, but I don't actually sit down and draw what I'm thinking about. I want to see what it feels like to use that creative energy the moment it arises. By doing this I'll be testing out another way of using my creativity. I'm very curious about how this change in the way I work will affect both my drawings and me. I am planning to continue my scheduled studio time, while also testing out this 'instant art' method. My productive obsession: for the whole month, every time I think of drawing something, I will immediately go to my easel and draw for a minimum of ten minutes."

Andrew explained, "I have spent many days obsessing over my obsession. Grand ideas have never frightened me. Staying focused long enough to complete them is more the problem. In the end it came down to five choices: a new large-scale musical on a historical subject, a smaller nonfiction musical, a new information website, my first novel, and a book about my family history. All these ideas are compelling to me, and I feel confident that each will get done in time. The new nonfiction musical is an old idea but won out because it has given me such trouble for so long. It won't go away, though I've done almost nothing on it. The difficulty has been trying to find an honest approach. I need a fresh approach for the material, and I want to expand the art form. It is the musical biography of a mid-twentieth-century figure. Biographies told as musical theater are challenging, particularly if the piece is original and not based on a film or book. Creating a sound that encapsulates a lifetime has also been difficult. My productive obsession: I throw down the gauntlet! I will obsess this piece into being."

Jennifer wrote, "I've been writing fiction for eight years, and during that time I've attended workshops and conferences, completed six manuscripts, honed my craft, studied the markets, and collected lots of rejections. I know the ropes. Currently I'm finishing up revisions on my latest manuscript. Feedback from my critique partners suggests that this could be the one that makes a publisher say yes. But lately I've been feeling that I've played this book too safe, that I need to do major revisions to make it more lively. Although I think the process of obsessing about letting it all hang out on the page will be scary, I have a gut feeling that it's the right thing for this book and the right thing for my growth as an author. My productive obsession: to learn how to make my latest manuscript big, bold, and fresh and to make those changes before sending it out to agents and editors."

Amber explained, "Using our hints for choosing productive obsessions, I found that certain of my current ideas met some of the criteria but that no idea met them all. Suddenly I realized that the idea of creating large-scale sculpture seemed to resonate with all the 'g's, although one sticking point was whether this choice would be congruent with my current self, since I haven't done any sculpture for nearly ten years. When I examined whether that desire was still valid, I became engaged and started obsessing about what mediums and materials to use. My heart began racing. I frequently experience these feelings when I get ideas for new paintings, but I could tell that sculpture on a larger scale was grander than doing another painting. It is also a gamble, since I am definitely not sure of the outcome. My productive obsession: to create large-scale sculpture."

Lilith wrote, "I knew right away what my obsession would be but gave myself overnight to test it. This morning it still rang true. Over the past year I've worked hard to build a body of paintings, and I was recently accepted into a gallery. I love my work, and each piece is a challenge, often scaring me by what it represents emotionally and symbolically. And I've been happy with that. However, I recently began to wonder if I needed to put more bite into my serene pieces. I remember years ago in art class a fellow student challenging me to use red. I was afraid of red then but slowly started using it — and I still use it only sparingly. Red has bite. Today I added a slight dash of coral to a painting I thought was finished, and it is so much better! I also drew some images of blood and knives, things that I never put into my paintings. In daily life my public persona is one of calmness and patience, and no one sees the edgy me except maybe the house spiders and the cats. My productive obsession: to put more bite into my art and really let loose!"

Celia wrote, "How did I arrive at my productive obsession, to create a series of sculptural fiber vessels? By going around and around on five options. I wrote them all down on separate pieces of paper, chose one at random, and then listened carefully to my internal dialogue as I read 'the answer.' Was I excited or disappointed, or did I want to choose again? When no decision came easily, I coached myself. First I wrote out a description of each option, including my fears and desires and any obstacles and problems. Then my internal coach asked for further clarification: What do I want to gain? What am I hoping will happen? and so on. Two options dropped away, and three remained strong. Then I noticed something. Friday I found myself gathering materials to start the vessel project. While my mind was still deciding, my body was preparing! And now I can't stop obsessing as the excitement builds."

Orient yourself in the direction of your productive obsession. There is no formula for arriving at that obsession; there is only the honest work of thinking through what project will serve you at this precise moment. Take all the time you need. Who knows, you may find yourself beginning to obsess even before you consciously realize that you have chosen.

AN OBSESSION
WITH RE-CREATING

Your obsession may drive you to create something, or it may drive you to preserve what has already been created. There is great value in personal creativity, and there is also great value in museum collections, heritage sites, and other conservation efforts. Consider Dr. Robert Hart's re-creative obsession: In 1967 he and his wife, Becky, bought two hundred acres in Hickory, North Carolina, imagining that they would create a wildlife rescue and retreat center.

Instead, the Harts have re-created an entire village, now known as the 1840 Carolina Village, which they've opened to the public for one day a year since 1985.

Dr. Hart, a physician and former Marine Corps fighter pilot, and his wife first created ponds and wildlife refuge areas on their acreage. But when one of Dr. Hart's patients suggested that they needed a historically authentic log cabin on the land and pointed the Harts toward one (the Hunsucker Cabin, circa 1840), they caught "cabin fever." The Hunsucker Cabin became the first of seventy authentically restored buildings, including churches, public houses, and a granary, which now comprise the 1840 Carolina Village. The Harts relied on leads from family, friends, and patients, and from sightings made by Dr. Hart as he flew his Cessna 150 over the surrounding area.

Dr. Hart would photograph his new acquisitions, number the logs at their joints, dismantle the structures, and carry them away on his old flatbed truck. According to journalist Nathan Moehlmann, today "each building, furnished according to its use, is in itself a museum, and Hart's wife, Becky, who has been instrumental in determining both the site of the buildings in the village as well as their interiors, has encouraged him to look now only for items that will round out the collections."

There is a productive obsession to fit every personality and every interest. There are productive obsessions for history buffs, born storytellers, inveterate collectors, librarians, lovers, adventurers, and homebodies. What's yours?

chapter ten

Meaning and Productive Obsessions

HOW DO WE DECIDE WHAT TO VALUE and where to make meaning? We make such decisions in the most obvious ways. We chat with ourselves about our passions and our principles; we sort through possible meaning investments; we discard those that feel too small, too boring, or too trivial; we spend real time thinking about how we want to manifest our life purposes and make ourselves proud. The process is precisely this simple — and precisely this difficult. Participants in my productive obsession group described their process of choosing productive obsessions that aligned with their meaning needs as follows.

Ann explained, "When I first started thinking about what I would like to productively obsess about, two specific projects sprang to mind, but I discarded them because I didn't feel that click of intuition that either was the right choice. Last year I turned forty, and I started to reflect on making meaning in my life. I have never quite figured out what I want to be when I grow up, and now that I am grown up, it feels a little like I've missed that train. I know there's a lot more to me than being a housewife — but what? Spending some quality time and energy really digging into what I want to do and making that happen clicked with me. It feels like exactly what I need to spend an entire month doing. My productive obsession: learning who I am and what I want, then finding meaningful work that connects to my intentions."

Nancy wrote, "I've been working on a dissertation on the New York Police Department and minorities for some time now. Choosing the dissertation to be my productive obsession seemed logical: it is certainly the project that I should be obsessing about right now. However, simply choosing my dissertation felt too easy and not on point. So I thought about it some more and discovered that what I really wanted to focus on was why I started this PhD program in the first place: to gain insight into the strained relationship between the NYPD and minorities. This core concern genuinely interests me, I believe it has all the 'g's,' and it feels meaningful. My productive obsession: to write a dissertation that provides insight into the strained relationship between the New York Police Department and minorities."

Loree explained, "For the last several years I've been employed doing social change work, which is my ideal job, but it requires hunting for grants and doing lots of fund-raising. I need to keep focusing on molding our work into fundable pieces, but this productive obsession opportunity feels like a chance to think about whether I'm making the best use of my skills. If I spend a little time each week thinking about what really needs doing in the world that only I can do, could that also end up being fundable? Might productive obsessing land me on a project that can be integrated into my ongoing work? My productive obsession: to figure out what I've learned that I can put out into the world. This may relate to what I've been doing so far, but I'm open to the possibility that it may point me in the direction of an even larger concern and an even grander project."

Marlene wrote, "I'm among a handful of women in a new field (well, really an old field that is being revived). We use different names for the field because so far we can't find one that we all agree on. We are variously known as Deathing Midwives, Home Funeral Guides, and Death Care Consultants. Our work has been performed quietly and under the radar. But all that changed when a state senator decided she needed to protect consumers from services like ours. She cast a wide net, and we have been caught in it. Now we're headed to the state capital to meet and greet, speak our passion, and build an association that we hope will attract other trades and services relating to alternative funerals. I see this as the place where I must make my meaning, even though it requires that I step out into a bright public light. My productive obsession: to learn how to help build an organization, all before the end of June. Yikes!"

Carla wrote, "I work a lot (maybe too much) in my day job and over the years have come to put that first and my own needs last. My personal writing is becoming safe, boring, and legalistic, and my internal censor is now ten feet tall ("You can't say that; you shouldn't notice that; oh, dear, people won't like it if you do that"). The culture at my day job is risk averse and that fault-finding, risk-identifying behavior is spilling into my life in general. How can I reach others with my writing if I'm not open to experiencing the world and not telling the truth in my work? My productive obsession: to loosen up and tell the truth."

Sara explained, "I've spent my life as a nonconformist,

following where the trail led, studying lots of things, including arts and consciousness, while exploring, traveling, and generally having a good time. More recently I've become a creativity coach and studied online marketing. I am now aching to give back, to contribute something of value to the world using my gifts. This has always been my Achilles' heel, making something out of what I've learned and experienced. The message to do something grown-up is echoing in my ears. It is time to step out of the student/child role and into a contributor/adult role. This is my biggest life challenge and one I am absolutely ready to meet. So the first part of my productive obsession is to understand what I intend to provide, and the second part is to create the accompanying website, products, and all the rest. This is how I will make my meaning."

I make my meaning — or else I don't. The same holds true for you. All that exists until I actively make personal meaning is the possibility of meaning and, while I wait to get started, the experience of emptiness. There is the possibility that I will experience the next hour as meaningful, a possibility that turns into a reality only if I make a certain kind of decision and a certain kind of investment. If I don't make that decision and that investment, I find myself going through the motions and wasting my precious time. We've all had that experience — for many of us, for far too much of the time.

How do you make meaning? By letting go of wondering what the universe wants of you, by letting go of the fear that nothing matters, and by announcing that you will make life mean exactly what you intend it to mean. This is an amazing, glorious, and triumphant announcement. The instant that you realize that meaning is not provided, as traditional belief systems teach, and that it is not absent, as nihilists feel, a new world of potential opens up for you. You've aimed yourself in a brilliant direction: the direction of your own creation.

You look forthrightly at the next hour, the next week, and the next month, and you make conscious decisions about what you intend to value and how you intend to spend your time. Your current productive obsession, and all your subsequent productive obsessions, is the fruit of this process of investing meaning. The phrase "investing meaning" does a nice job of capturing the flavor of what making meaning entails. You say to yourself, "I am investing meaning in my idea for a nonprofit," you turn your mind in that direction and you move from the half-meaninglessness of mere interest to the meaningfulness of authentic engagement.

Step back and ask yourself, "Where do I want to make my meaning?" Conceptualize this process of naming and nurturing productive obsessions as integral to the way you value life and manifest your purpose. A productive obsession is not just a cool idea, an intriguing pastime, or a piece of mental stimulation. It is the answer to the question, "How can I make myself proud?" You decide what to value, you throw yourself into the fray, and the result is a productive obsession. Indeed, isn't authentic living exactly the birthing and nurturing of an endless series of productive obsessions?

ADRIFT ON THE OCEANS

Maybe oceans provide you with an existential spark. Your life feels more meaningful when you're by the sea — or on it. That is all well and good: But how might you translate that existential resonance into some actual meaning-making? You could become a merchant sailor; you could relocate to a seaside town; you could periodically cruise. And if none of those pursuits seemed rich enough? Well, you could go whole hog and become an oceanographer. Wouldn't some productive obsession like the one that gripped Curtis Ebbesmeyer almost surely follow?

Ebbesmeyer is consumed with tracking and collecting flotsam. Flotsam — described as human-created "stuff" of potential value that has found its way overboard, usually as a result of an accident or a weather-related incident — is Ebbesmeyer's special province. His fascination with flotsam has a purpose beyond the mere recording of found items; he is particularly curious about what tracking flotsam can reveal about the mysteries of ocean currents. With his coauthor, journalist Eric Scigliano, Ebbesmeyer has written *Flotsametrics and the Floating World*, a compendium on flotsam that includes some amazing stories of found items.

His book also includes explanations of how tracking debris has helped him discern patterns in the oceans' currents. To draw in and keep beach lovers engaged with his flotsam obsession, Ebbesmeyer issues a Web-based "Beachcombers Alert" several times a year in which he tracks ocean container spills, responds to readers' questions, and mobilizes flotsam-collecting volunteers worldwide. In addition, he hosts "the radio program *Flotsam Hour*, in which listeners call in with interesting flotsam (like *Antiques Road-show* for ocean currents)."

Making personal meaning sometimes entails round-the-clock work on behalf of a cause, full exhaustion in the service of a creative project, and hard mental labor as you craft the authentic thing to say or to do. Even very productive people harbor a primitive fear of expending their human capital on work of their own choosing, saving exhaustion and overwork for their "day job." Decide to spend your capital on your own meaning-making needs. To the world it may look as if you are merely collecting rubber ducks and runaway sneakers at the water's edge. You, however, know better: you are investing in the earth's oceans.

chapter eleven

Your Productive Obsession Checklist

P URSUING A PRODUCTIVE OBSESSION requires more than naming it and hoping for the best. It requires that you channel your thinking in new ways, fight off lassitude, cheerlead for your obsession, and stick with it when the going gets tough. Here are ten tips for nurturing your productive obsession and incorporating it into your everyday life.

Tip 1. Mean It.

It is easy to say "I am going to obsess a school into existence" or "I intend to devote myself to medical research." Saying things is easy. It is harder to mean what we say. To mean something, as opposed to saying something, is to demand of ourselves that we move to a courageous place that we rarely occupy. We are obliged to stand up straighter, marshal our will, look reality in the eye, and rise up like a hero. It is hard to do this if we do not genuinely love the thing we have chosen, but even if real love is present, it is still hard. Manifest your courage and really mean it when you announce your productive obsession.

Tip 2. Own It.

Accept what you have wrought. It is one thing to mean it when you say that you intend to start a business or master string theory. It's another thing to accept the consequences of your intentions. If you do not fully accept that you have embarked on what may be a taxing adventure with all sorts of predictable and unexpected obstacles, then when one of those obstacles appears you will balk, lose energy, and maybe even stop completely. Accept that you have made work for yourself, work that no one asked you to make. You made the decision, you set the bar, you offered up your neurons. Own that decision.

Tip 3. Strategize.

A productive obsession provokes all sorts of mental states — euphoria when something goes brilliantly, irritation when you feel thwarted, fatigue after hours of mental struggle, excitement as one idea leads to another. What strategy will you employ when you feel thwarted? When you feel exhausted? When you're excited and tempted to overcelebrate? Brainstorms produce psychological and emotional states that require our attention. Have you grown a little too agitated? Know what to do. (A hot shower works wonders.) Have you grown sad that you've hit a dead end? Know what to do. (Maybe it's time for Belgian chocolate.) Invent some new strategies and remember the ones that have proven effective in the past.

Tip 4. Plan.

How will your productive obsession and the rest of your life fit together? You can't plan for every contingency, but you can certainly plan for the eventualities that are known to you. Do you have a day job? Plan that when you leave it, you will really leave it. The second you punch out, you will stop thinking about your co-worker's last rude comment or tomorrow's sales meeting. Do you have an upcoming family vacation? Plan how to steal time from it for your obsession. Make yourself available to your family all day long — except for those two hours while the family recuperates from its trip to the theme park. Plan when you will say yes to your obsession and when you will say no to it — and plan to say yes more often than no.

Tip 5. Stretch.

You are making your life that much busier by adding a productive obsession. That addition will amount to a real stretch as your days get longer and your mind gets wilder. Get ready to stretch. If you've decided to tackle a project that is larger, riskier, or more complex than anything you've tackled before, mentally prepare for your experience by visualizing your efforts. See yourself pushing hard, getting exhausted, clawing your way up that last thousand feet, and congratulating yourself at the top of the mountain. Expect the mental and emotional equivalent of aches and pains: this is not the calm, measured stretching that a runner engages in before she starts her first marathon but the whole-body, whole-mind stretching required of her for the race. If your productive obsession requires great stretching, get ready for it.

Tip 6. Economize.

We possess an astronomical number of neurons, but we need all of them. It is bad economics to spend a hundred million neurons on a worry, another hundred million on a doubt, and a full billion plotting how to get revenge on the bus driver who glared at us. To be profligate with our natural resources is wasteful and dangerous. Do not countenance the thoughts that steal your neurons and serve no useful purpose. Unnecessary expenditures will cost you a portion of your brilliance.

Tip 7. Regulate.

A productive obsession stirs up the mind. Picture a snow globe and a can of soda being shaken. In the first case, the snow settles calmly of its own accord: the snow globe is designed that way. In the second case it is very hard, sometimes verging on impossible, to open the can without courting an explosion. You want to be a snow globe and not a soda can. You want to self-regulate. Your first goal is to adequately shake yourself up, since that shaking is proof that you've bitten into something worth chewing. Your second goal is to remain in charge of your brainstorm.

Tip 8. Switch Gears.

Much of the difficulty in pursing a productive obsession is how exhausting it can feel to repeatedly switch gears between your normal life and your obsessive life. Therefore, one important goal is to learn how to switch gears effortlessly, so that, for instance, no time is wasted and no internal drama created as you leave your day job and return to your symphony. Imagine that you have — or are — a flawless transmission system, whisper-quiet and beautifully constructed, that allows you to move efficiently through the day, revving up to obsess and revving down to peel potatoes or chat with your mate.

Tip 9. Monitor.

Have you been running too hot and driving yourself in the direction of danger? Take a break from your obsession. Have you been running too cold, rarely getting to your obsession and disappointing yourself in the process? Return to the tips in this section. Imagine that you are hooked up to a futuristic machine that monitors your meaning needs, your energy level, your responsibilities, and your passions and that provides you with second-by-second information and instructions, telling you when to take a break from your obsession, when to turn a whole week over to it, and everything else you need to know to maintain your mental health and your productivity. Check the readings regularly.

Tip 10. Recommit.

The best of life demands a daily — even a moment-by-moment — recommitment to our ideals, intentions, and efforts. We are divided creatures capable of either whiling away years or achieving our maximum. Each of us has that do-nothing, watch-a-little-more-television place in our heart and that think-intensely and work-well place, but the latter is harder to engage. The life of your productive obsession depends on your constant recommitment to your ideals, intentions, and efforts. This recommitment sounds like "I am doing this, damn it!" Let your moment-by-moment recommitment have some fierceness. The instant your mind produces one of its little stories about why you ought to abandon your productive obsession — because you can't succeed, because you feel tired, because a storm is coming — shout, "No!" Shout and recommit.

Once you've thought through the consequences of committing to each of these ten tips, put a check mark where you agree:

❑ I mean it.   ❑ I will economize.
❑ I own it.   ❑ I will regulate.
❑ I will strategize.   ❑ I will switch gears.
❑ I will plan.   ❑ I will monitor.
❑ I will stretch.   ❑ I will recommit.

COLD OUT?

The natural obstacles that arise to everything worth doing prevent people from pursuing their passions. This is one of the main reasons that you want to move from "mere interest" to "productive obsession." You want to up the emotional and psychological ante, so that if it is freezing outside you simply bundle up and get out there with your obsession. For sometimes it will be freezing out; witness the productive obsession of Captain William Hutchinson.

Living in the 1700s, English-born Captain Hutchinson spent his entire life connected to the sea. Having been a sailor, a sea merchant, and an officer in the Royal Navy, Hutchinson exhibited a love of the sea that led him to think creatively about ways to improve the lives of those whose livelihood depended on the sea. Hutchinson invented the mirrors used in lighthouse lamps and designed an oil-fired light source that in 1763 transformed lighthouses into far-reaching beacons for sailors and greatly improved their safety at sea. In 1776, when he was the dock master and water bailiff for Liverpool, Hutchinson established the first — and only, until 1803 — lifeboat serving a harbor in the British Isles.

As for one of his sustained, productive obsessions, for nearly thirty years Hutchinson made daily records of the heights and times of high and low tide, which meant venturing to the shore several times a day, every day of the year, regardless of the weather. His data has provided clear evidence that since the eighteenth century sea level has been rising and that this trend has accelerated during the latter half of the twentieth century, a result in keeping with contemporary hypotheses about the disastrous effects of greenhouse gases. Hutchinson's data, the result of his productive obsession and regularly collected in the bitter cold of a British winter, has proven crucial for the study of climatic change.

chapter twelve

Early Daze

Y OU MAY EXPERIENCE DRAMATIC UPS AND DOWNS during your first days of productive obsessing. It is typical to start with a bang on day one and to end up whimpering on day two; to find day one difficult, day two inspiring, and day three a bust; to attend to your obsession for only a few minutes when you had planned to devote hours to it; and so on. In the face of what are sometimes steep downs, it is not unusual for new productive obsessors to doubt the rightness of their choice, their ability to integrate their obsession into their life, and even the utility of obsessing. When such pressing doubts and difficulties arise, many new obsessors give up.

For others, their choice retains its feeling of rightness, but they find that they have precious little interest in or energy for their new obsession. They still like it — but they're already not attending to it. You would think that an obsession would be more gripping than that! How can you claim to be obsessed and by day two act as if you're not even interested? How can you thoughtfully create a plan for fitting your obsession into your life and find yourself incapable of keeping to your plan a mere twenty-four hours later? Was it really a productive obsession or only wishful thinking or a passing fancy? Such are the questions that pester new productive obsessors.

Miriam, a participant in my productive obsession group, explained, "This has been hair-raisingly hard. I got everything work related done this weekend to the point of forgetting about my chosen obsession and even about all my personal interests. Then I had a prolonged internal battle with myself for a few days. Trying to implement this obsession is bringing me face-to-face with all my negative attitudes and tendencies. My ingrained resistance to doing big work is fighting hard to keep me from obsessing. I just hope it isn't this grueling all month! But as hard as this is for me — and on me — I really believe that fostering this obsession, and wrestling with my gremlins so that the obsession finally dominates them, is necessary and that my terrible struggle will prove worthwhile."

Marcia reported, "After a great obsessive weekend, I have to admit that I really had a bad day today. I did not sleep well, so I already started off the day in a foul mood. I felt tired and unproductive throughout the day — as if there was this big cloud in my head that obstructed me from thinking — and then I started obsessing about my lack of productivity. I tried to get out of this mood by going to the gym and then starting again, but it didn't really work. I'm noticing that once you start off unproductive, it often stays that way throughout the day. I am shifting gears now, but only into PARK. This will be an early night for me! Maybe tomorrow will be better."

Productive obsessing is a marathon, not a sprint. You might think it's a sprint, because of the bursts of energy that we associate with our most fiery thinking. But actually such sprints are the exception. The rule is that we have many miles to go to build our business, write our novel, or complete our research. Bruce, a member of my productive obsession group, provided another metaphor. He likened the experience of his early days of obsessing to Formula One racing rather than NASCAR racing. In a NASCAR race, the cars go fast all the time. In Formula One racing, the shape of the circuit prevents drivers from traveling at constant high speeds. They are going fast by highway standards but must vary their speed by as much as a hundred miles an hour, downshifting to 120 miles an hour to negotiate curves and revving up to 220 miles an hour on straightaways.

This Formula One metaphor nicely captures the life of a productive obsession. We are not always tackling it at the highest possible speed, since the life of the obsession dictates whether we are negotiating curves or flying down a straightaway. But we are moving along at a decent clip, paying attention, switching gears, and keeping our eye on the road. We are engaged, goal-oriented, and dealing with what is likely mounting pressure. The race is on, and we are responding.

Bruce explained, "It is rare for me to openly acknowledge or give myself permission to have an obsession, especially publicly. But the work we did leading up to the starting line helped me to focus on my obsession. On day one I did what I said I would do: I went straight to my project first thing in the morning. By lunch I had made real progress. Late in the day I was mowing the lawn and still thinking about my project. Then I ate dinner, expecting to go back to the studio to wrap up a good first day. Instead I turned on the television, quickly fell asleep, woke up thinking that I could still go work on my project . . . and discovered that I couldn't.

"Day two started with that uh-oh feeling. I thought to myself that I had too much to do: housecleaning, work on the car, et cetera. But I felt uncomfortable about not doing something on behalf of my obsession. What I noticed this morning as I reread our tip sheet is that I need to adjust my transmission to allow for a smoother switching of gears. This is good to know at the beginning of the race to avoid blowing up midway. I know that this is exactly the right obsession for me to test-drive for the month — I just have to learn how to run this race."

Expect everything from ennui to whirlwinds as you begin your first days of productive obsessing. You might want to create your own metaphor that captures something of the special dynamism of this adventure. Birthing a productive obsession and seeing it through to its conclusion is not like attending to everyday business. It requires more of you, and it rewards you better. Is it a marathon? A Formula One race? How would you characterize it?

INTO THE SWAMP

Your early days of productive obsessing may be filled with equal measures of excitement and resistance. Resistance to your own ideas can feel like slogging through a swamp, as the very size, complexity, and reality of your ideas confront you and bog you down. Keep your eye on the fascination and not on the difficult footing! If you can manage that, you may get results like Susan Orlean's.

Journalist Susan Orlean became fascinated with the true story of John Laroche, who in the mid-1990s was arrested in Florida for poaching rare orchids with the intent of cloning and selling them on the underground orchid collectors' market. Orlean journeyed to South Florida to interview Laroche and ended up "shadowing Laroche and exploring the odd, passionate world of orchid fanatics," and spending two years constructing a story that went well beyond anything she could have imagined when she was first drawn to the scene.

With a passion for her story, Orlean immersed herself in the swampy environment of orchid thieves and came out with *The Orchid Thief*, her bestselling book on which the 2002 movie *Adaptation* is based. In the process of writing the book, Orlean "learned the history of orchid collecting, discovered an odd pattern of plant crimes in Florida, and spent time with Laroche's partners, a tribe of Seminole Indians who are still at war with the United States."

A journalist may have a strong intuition that she is on to a great story, but in her first days of research she can't yet know if her story will pan out and turn into something really fascinating. The same is true for you: in the early days of your productive obsession it may be hard to know if your idea is genuinely worth pursuing. Give it time! Will yourself knee-deep into the swamp, where alligators and great ideas live, and opt to believe that the result will be more than worth the slog.

chapter thirteen

Risk

I T IS NO SURPRISE that Fyodor Dostoyevsky, a writer with magnificent productive obsessions, was also a gambling addict. There is an intimate relationship between productive obsessions and a risk-taking temperament. You skillfully name your productive obsession; you're certain that you mean it when you say that you intend to birth this business, symphony, or scientific theory; and yet all you manage to do is obsess about obsessing. What happened? It might be that you picked an unsuitable obsession. It might be that your obsession wasn't as interesting as you'd hoped it would be. But what's most likely is that you are not accustomed to risk-taking.

To productively obsess, you must be easy with taking the risks that accompany difficult projects. What are those risks? That choosing this obsession was a mistake. That you won't succeed. That you'll disappoint yourself (again) or that the world will disappoint you (again). Unless you're in the habit of taking such risks automatically, so that risk-taking is not even an issue for you, you will have to train yourself to consciously announce that you are about to risk. You must put the idea of risk on the table and then fiercely embrace it.

Consider the following three distinct states. First, there is the state of pursuit, where we find ourselves trying, say, to figure out how gravitation works or how to make use of that folk melody we heard as a child. We may not be putting pen to graph paper or to composition paper yet, but we are actively pursuing something and know that's what we're doing. Even though no excellent conclusion is guaranteed us, we are nevertheless trying. We have accepted the risk and we are off and running, even though to the world we may look as if we're just sitting there thinking.

Then there is the state of action, where we find ourselves meeting with investors in search of business funding or putting words on the page in the service of our novel. Our productive obsession has turned into productive action: we are doing what needs to be done, maybe in a stress-free way, maybe in a pressurized way, but either way we are hard at work and taking relevant action. We have accepted the risk, and we look engaged and active.

Then there is a third state, the state of avoidance. We are not really obsessing about our idea, only about our doubts and worries. We aren't thinking, "How does gravity work?" We're thinking, "How can somebody with an IQ of only 135 solve such a problem?" We aren't thinking, "How can I use that folk melody in the third movement of my symphony?" We're thinking, "Who in her right mind would compose a symphony nowadays?" We haven't embraced the risk inherent in interesting projects, and we're secretly hoping for guarantees. We are not off and running: we are stuck and spinning.

You must remind yourself that making meaning entails unavoidable risk. The phrase "making meaning investments" nicely captures the idea of risk, and it is a phrase you may want to adopt to remind yourself of what you're attempting when you opt to obsess productively. You're taking your precious capital, your time, your energy, and your neurons, and investing them in an undertaking with zero guarantees. You aren't assured of even a marginal reward on this investment, a nice little 2 or 3 percent return. You are guaranteed nothing.

In the world of productive obsessing, the risk you are taking is on the order of stock speculation in a shaky market. You are speculating that you will find a vaccine, one that perhaps doesn't exist. You are speculating that your new painting style will move painting forward, a high-risk gamble. You are speculating that your thoughts and feelings can coalesce into a grand one-woman performance piece that someone will stage and produce, a long-odds endeavor. You are speculating.

The better you understand to what extent you are speculating with this ambitious novel, business venture, or political ambition, the more likely it is that you can move to pursuit and action. Factor in the danger, nominate yourself as the hero of your story, and mount your steed. Take the risk that your project may not prove as important as you had hoped. Take the risk that it will prove exactly as important as you had hoped, taxing you with its difficulty and troubling you by its felt significance. Take the risk that running for office will prove exactly as stressful as you fear it will be. Take the risk that the months of devotion to your new business are worth the effort, even if the business produces red ink. Take the risk.

Some people do not experience this sort of stretching as risk. Whether it is because it is built into their DNA or for some other reason, folks in this position do not have to talk themselves into a willingness to risk. They take on even the biggest projects without blinking. It isn't so much that they embrace the risk they feel; they do not experience their choices as risky. If you are not one of these folks — or are no longer one of these folks, having become fearful in the course of living — you will need to settle your nerves and talk yourself into a solid understanding of the importance of risk. You might put it this way: "Nothing ventured, nothing gained." Whatever language you use, get the matter of risk on the table. The second you say, "This is risky, but I really don't mind," you will move from avoidance to pursuit and action.

RISKING ALICE

What if you fear that the productive obsession you're about to choose is odd, silly, pointless, or self-indulgent? What if you're obsessing about turning the fallen leaves on your property into an enormous "eco-wreath" but can't help wondering whether that amounts to eco-art or childishness? What if you harbor the hunch that your current research serves no useful purpose except to fill the pages of some specialized journal? What if you fall in love with *Alice in Wonderland*, as the composer David Del Tredici did, and decide to spend a lifetime in Alice's pursuit? Should you indulge that odd passion or fend it off?

Del Tredici's obsession began when he played the White Rabbit in a grammar school musical version of *Alice in Wonderland*. When he read Martin Gardner's *The Annotated Alice*, it got further inflamed, and it simmered for three decades. Obsessed with Lewis Carroll, *Alice in Wonderland*, and the actual Alice whom Lewis Carroll knew, Del Tredici composed *Pop-Pourri*, a half-hour "cantata of the sacred and profane" juxtaposing passages from *Alice's Adventures in Wonderland* with the Litany of the Blessed Virgin; an *Alice Symphony*, comprising "Illustrated Alice" and "In Wonderland"; *Vintage Alice*, a mad tea party fantasy; *Child Alice*, a long work containing the march "Triumphant Alice"; *Haddocks' Eyes*, a symphonic song based on the works of Lewis Carroll and Thomas Moore; *Dum Dee Tweedle*, a one-act opera based on the "Tweedledum and Tweedledee" chapter of *Through the Looking Glass*; and more.

This is odd, of course. But is it too odd? With respect to your own "Alice," only you can say. If you want to say yes to your Alice, accept the risks involved and get your battle cry ready, maybe one on the order of "More Alice, please!"

chapter fourteen

Commitment

MAYBE YOU'VE DREAMED ABOUT OBSESSING over a certain problem: let's call it Newton's Last Stand (NLS), a problem in solid geometry that no mathematician has come close to solving. You know that NLS could consume you — if only you weren't so easily distracted. You love NLS with a passion, you search the Internet every day to make sure that no one has solved it, and you get goose bumps when you think about adding your name to the pantheon of mathematicians who've solved knotty math puzzles as gorgeous as NLS. NLS could be yours! — yet you seem incapable of getting a grip on your mind and paying NLS any serious attention.

You are so easily distracted that you find it hard to concentrate on NLS even for a few seconds at a time. You get a little too hot; that distracts you. You remember that your subscription to

Scientific American is running out; that distracts you. A garbage truck rumbles by; that distracts you. Your cat appears; that distracts you. Soon it will be time for dinner; that distracts you. The afternoon that you set aside for biting into NLS is productive for maybe five minutes all together — the rest of the time is mayhem.

What's wrong? You certainly know how to concentrate. You can read even the most abstruse book in one sitting. You can sit through whole operas. You can follow the most complicated mathematical arguments. You can do math puzzles for hours on end without looking up. When it comes to NLS, however, it's as if you have bees in your underwear. Just thinking about NLS gets you fidgeting. A minute in, and you're ready to jump overboard. What's going on?

What's happened is that you haven't really committed. Productive obsessors are committed and therefore hard to distract. They don't notice the truck rumbling by, the cat changing positions on the sofa, the heat or the cold, weeds overtaking their garden, or the impending demise of their magazine subscription. They are entranced. They are really grappling with their NLS, deeply lost in their fictional world, completely taken with the composition emerging on the canvas before their eyes. It isn't that they are ignoring the truck rumbling by; they don't hear it. It isn't that they are fighting off thoughts about their magazine subscription; they aren't having them. It isn't that they are trying not to be distracted; they simply aren't.

The matter isn't constitutional. I run workshops for writers who would call themselves easily distractible and who fail to productively obsess to such an extent that they don't write for months on end. In my weeklong workshops, after virtually no introduction or preparation, these blocked writers sit quietly and write prolifically hour after hour, not allowing anything to distract them. Why? Because I suggest it is possible. Because I remind them that meaning exists only when they make it. Because I sit there doing absolutely nothing except holding the group intention to write. And because, if something like a potential distraction occurs — if a truck rumbles by — I laugh and remind them that they do not need to be distracted. They look up, nod, and continue writing. This goes on for a whole week. At the end of that time they have ten or fifteen thousand words written.

At home, unaccustomed to biting into their work and quite accustomed to finding reasons not to work, they allow the slightest breeze to distract them. In the workshop, invited to bite into their work and stripped of reasons to avoid their work, they write for hours on end. The same person who sought distraction at home rejects distraction at the workshop. You are that kind of person. You aren't constitutionally an easily distracted person. You are a person who sometimes seeks distractions and who sometimes rejects distractions. You seek them when you feel uncommitted; you reject them when you feel committed. Most people fail to commit and, as a result, opt for distractions. Far fewer people commit.

You can halt a brainstorm with a feather. All you have to do is keep looking up or looking away. All you have to do is take no real interest in your own ideas. All you have to do is secretly doubt that your efforts matter. All you have to do is get in the habit of calling yourself "easily distractible" and buy every available distraction. If you want to make absolutely sure that you will not be able to concentrate, all you have to do is not commit. That will guarantee that the slightest change in barometric pressure will distract you.

Picture the Ohio River where it runs between Indiana and Kentucky. It is wide, racing, and formidable — but at your swimming best you could cross it. Imagine yourself standing on the Indiana bank in your wetsuit, greased and amiable, ready to swim to Kentucky, where something excellent awaits you, some sweet kisses, the solution to a great mystery, a dry-aged steak and onion rings, the Holy Grail. Imagine that over there, on the Kentucky shore, is something you really want — but between you and it is that rushing river. How cold it looks! And that tanker edging this way — it could cut you in half. And when did you last eat? — isn't that your stomach rumbling? Because you're focusing on the difficulty of the crossing and not on the Holy Grail awaiting you in Kentucky, everything distracts you.

As you stand there, either you have decided to cross the river or you haven't. You know the difference. You know the difference between dipping your toes in the water and jumping in. You know the difference between standing at the water's edge, judging the enormous distance between you and that distant shore, and diving in, indifferent to the distance. You know the difference. If you treat your obsession in the former way, with only your toes in the water, the solution to Newton's Last Stand is bound to elude you. If you treat your obsession in the latter way, as a complete commitment, you have a shot at getting to Kentucky.

Perhaps you have some toes in the water but you are still very near the shore, afraid of immersing yourself and unwilling to commit to the dangers of the crossing. Productive obsessors, whether or not they enjoy the swim, really want to get to Kentucky. Over there, on that distant shore, is something that matters to them, the solution to Newton's Last Stand, their *War and Peace*, something, and they jump in, maybe thrilled or maybe anxious, but in any event committed, their momentum taking them in the direction of Kentucky.

If you are only dipping your toes in the water and adamantly resisting the plunge, one honking goose flying overhead will distract you completely. Jump in. If you really jump in, you will discover that you are not a distractible person. That narrative you may be telling yourself about how easily you get distracted is a false one. Distractibility is a symptom and not a personality trait. If you are waiting for a guarantee before letting go of the near shore, you will remain there forever. Forget about guarantees: opt for commitment.

It is natural and even inevitable that a 7.6 earthquake would break your concentration. But idle thoughts about dinner or the weather should not. Worries about what tomorrow might bring and guilt about what yesterday brought should not. A cloud passing across the sun or a curtain fluttering in the breeze should not. If small events like these regularly break your concentration, you are not immersed in your work, you aren't obsessing, you haven't jumped in yet, and you haven't committed. To switch metaphors, you are on the sidelines and not in the game.

Maybe your idea bores you. That will make it hard for you to jump in. Maybe your idea overwhelms you. That will make it hard for you to jump in. Maybe your idea mystifies you. That will make it hard for you to jump in. Maybe your history of working small and not large haunts you. That will make it hard for you to jump in. Maybe you just can't find the switch to throw that will move you to commitment. Then stop everything and hunt for that switch.

IMMERSED IN INDIA

What does a decades-long commitment look like? Consider Japanese architect Takeo Kamiya's productive obsession with the architecture of India. Kamiya first traveled to India in 1976 for a three-month visit and has repeatedly returned ever since. From the first moment he caught sight of a traditional wooden temple, Kamiya fell in love with the design and proportions of India's buildings and historical sites.

At a time when most of his architect peers were traveling to the West, Kamiya chose to explore the birthplace of the Buddha. Although he had no guidebooks, no knowledge of Indian languages, and very little money, he decided that he would compile drawings and photographs of India's architecture for his Japanese compatriots who, unless they could afford to travel to India, had little access to its glorious beauty.

In 2003 Kamiya's book *The Guide to the Architecture of the Indian Subcontinent* was translated into English and became available in India and throughout the world. Gerard da Cunha, Indian architect and publisher of the English edition, speaks admiringly of Kamiya's obsession: "Looking at the Herculean effort it must have taken for one man to put together such a book, one can only imagine the kind of motivation and consistency it took," adding, "I wish I had a book like this when I was a student of architecture."

Commitment is not an ice-cold sort of thing, a victory of discipline over devotion, a win for the head over the heart. Commitment and love are partners: you will travel over any dusty road and ascend any mountain pass in pursuit of the next startling building to record if you've fallen in love and grown obsessive. Do not think of commitment as the equivalent of the Ohio River in winter. Think of it as hot and sunlit, like tropical waters perfect for snorkeling.

chapter fifteen

One-Week Reports

I ASK PARTICIPANTS in my productive obsession group to report on their first-week progress. Here are six reports:

Bob explained, "It felt very productive test-driving this obsession over the first week. Here are a few things I've noticed. Sometimes I allowed the obsession to be foremost in my mind, but at other times I had to insist that it not be the primary thought pattern. Then sometimes it would come blasting in and claim time of its own, regardless of when and where I was. Some of the swiftest progress occurred in this phase. Lots of times there was a kind of 'fear rush' present, fear that the obsession was too big, that I made a mistake in choosing it, and that I'm not really up to it. At other times the fear seemed to be that I was playing with fire and that this relatively controlled obsession would lead me in the direction of being completely overwhelmed by all the other obsessions awaiting their turn. I feel a sense of danger;

but having acknowledged and made a commitment to this particular obsession provides me with a way to say yes to whatever feelings show up."

Samantha wrote, "My first week wasn't as productive as I'd planned. I knew that my workweek was going to be extra busy, but it was even busier than I had anticipated. Still, I found that my mental focus was very much on my writing, even though I couldn't physically put pen to paper. As an added bonus, all that thinking about the writing gave me a giant shove in a direction I've wanted to go in for several years but haven't allowed myself to go in because of fear and uncertainty. I want to make the leap to writing and teaching (writing workshops and creativity classes) full-time, but I never let myself take the first steps because I am afraid I won't be able to make a career of it. But this week I'm realizing that my fears about long-range possibilities are holding me back from my writing. So, while I am keeping my current obsession, I am also seeing what long-range additions to the obsession I want to make that will (I hope) lead me to the life I want. I feel excited, and scared, and uncertain. But alive."

Michael explained, "I've been paralyzed by the sheer number of articles I've accumulated in pursuit of my doctorate in cognitive science. You would think that as a student of cognitive science I would have a better grip on my own mind — but no! I've even feared that I would have to drop out because I haven't been able to move from mountains of research to a clear, clean, doable — and also interesting and grand — dissertation topic. I've had ideas, but such small ones that they bore me the instant I have them. And the big ideas seem completely out of reach.

"This week I made the conscious decision not to do one

more lick of research and to buckle down and obsess a dissertation topic into existence. Monday was horrible. Tuesday was horrible. And Wednesday was even worse, as my demons howled away at me. Then on Thursday something happened. I actually got quiet and started thinking. It is a very strange experience to notice that you haven't really been thinking all these many years of school — that you've been avoiding thinking. My dissertation topic didn't become clear on Thursday, but I saw its ghostly outline, and I have some hope that it will become clear now that I have committed to thinking. What an odd concept, to finally commit to thinking after almost twenty years in school."

Alice reported, "My stated obsession about art, nature, and place has turned into an obsession with maps! Yes, maps — cartographic, artistic, and metaphorical. I'm having a great time reading, finding more books, playing with ideas, watching things unfold, and getting excited by it all. Yesterday I actually claimed some hours from my workday without feeling guilty! I am smitten with the idea of maps. At this stage I'd say I am in the state of pursuit, with only a little action, but at least I've found my way out of the state of avoidance."

Sophia explained, "About two years ago I started an Internet-based business with my husband and while we've had many successes with the business, generating revenue has not been one of them. We kept chasing advertisers and entering into deals that fell apart almost as soon as we sewed them up, because we could not really produce the results that the advertisers expected. So I've been obsessing about revenue for two years — but not really productively. I was like a rat trapped in a cage, clawing at revenue, and had no freedom to think about changing our revenue model.

"I decided to define *productive obsession* as 'deep, out-of-the-box thinking' and to give myself permission to toss out our revenue model if that's what was needed. This week has been completely thrilling! I discovered that the second I let go of my attachment to our advertising-based revenue model I felt this enormous freedom, rather than the fear I presumed I would feel. Tons of new ideas rushed into my brain, and I had to pursue two or three of them. One of them is leading the pack and quite likely will become our new revenue model. I have to do more research and make sure that I'm really on the right track, but I think that I am. This must be the very essence of productively obsessing!"

Alan reported, "What a week this has been! I've managed to produce a great deal of work, and, more important, 'big picture' issues for my project are coming together. The weekend was quite productive, and I kept to my plan of writing and reading. Monday, although I expected to be tired, as soon as I sat down my pen flew. I was quite worn out on Tuesday and decided to rest. On Wednesday I had a very full workday at the office and an evening meeting as well. I did a little reading but not much else. This morning I woke early, and two fresh solutions to plot problems appeared. I've filled my office with images of my subject, which I think is helping, and I'm thinking about the project a great deal. I'm not sure whether or not that's obsessing, but whatever it is, it's a great improvement! I'm still having trouble rising extra early, but I'm working later, so I'm not being hard on myself about not rising at the crack of dawn. So far, so good. On to week two!"

Your first week of productive obsessing may bring you face-to-face with your most tenacious, self-sabotaging behaviors and your fiercest demons. It may also open the door to riveting thinking and provide sudden solutions to your most intractable problems. Very likely, it may prove a mixture of both as you marshal your resources, look your resistance square in the eye, and commit to grandeur. No matter how it turns out, congratulate yourself if you showed up even a little.

ARTISTS OBSESSING

I have a special love for the way that visual artists obsess. We are constantly bombarded by visual stimuli, so a profound task of the visual artist is to create something "different from" all that already-existing stimuli, something that will speak to us through the hubbub of endless visual excitation. What do the productive obsessions of visual artists sound like? Here are a dozen:

1. "These landscapes of water and reflections have become an obsession. It's quite beyond my powers at my age, and yet I want to succeed in expressing what I feel." — CLAUDE MONET

2. "I wear myself out trying to render the orange trees so that they're not stiff but like those I saw by Botticelli in Florence. It's a dream that won't come true." — BERTHE MORISOT

3. "The creative habit is like a drug. The particular obsession changes, but the excitement, the thrill of your creation lasts." — HENRY MOORE

4. "A day without painting, or at least thinking of

something to paint, is a day without breathing." — LUZ
MARIA PEREZ

5. "It's three o'clock in the morning, your back hurts, your arm hurts, you've been in there for ten hours, and there are no sounds except for the occasional fire truck. Finally, you put the brush down and ask yourself, 'Man, what am I doing here?'" — JOHN ALEXANDER

6. "Painting seems to be my obsession. I feel some resentment at all the other things in life that take me away from my studio. This obsession constantly judges all other calls on my time and energy." — SUE COWAN

7. "I have, at times, been absorbed in my work to the point of complete self-oblivion. Once I worked for thirty-six hours without a break to complete exhaustion; and while I was in the middle of it I didn't even notice." — ALTON S. TOBEY

8. "The painter's obsession with his subject is all that he needs to drive him to work." — LUCIAN FREUD

9. "I'm a painter who paints day in and day out, from morning till evening." — GUSTAV KLIMT

10. "I don't see how you can create and not have the feeling that it is the most important, all-consuming thing." — GRACE HARTIGAN

11. "When you start to work you don't want to leave, you don't want to eat, you don't want to sleep." — HUI LIN LIU

12. "The cypresses are always occupying my thoughts." — VINCENT VAN GOGH

chapter sixteen

Mere Interest or Passionate Interest?

I AM MILDLY INTERESTED IN CHESS and occasionally play a game on the computer. I am passionately interested in human nature. I am mildly interested in jazz and enjoy listening to jazz on long road trips. I am passionately interested in the ideas of existentialism. I am mildly interested in the history of painting and sometimes read about the birth of abstractionism. I am passionately interested in how tyrants use language to sell their tyrannies. Many things interest me, but some are mere interests and others fuel brainstorms.

It is vital that a person who has decided to turn the seeds of interest into full-fledged productive obsessions learn to distinguish between those things that merely interest him and those things that really interest him. If he can't make some sensible distinctions, he may try to build brainstorms in places of insufficient interest. If, say, his "love of nature" amounts to little

more than a fondness for walking in the nearby woods in good
weather, it is unlikely that a brainstorm resides in the direction
of "exploring a love of nature." Better that he find some inner
place of fire and passion.

How do you know if you are merely interested or if you are
seriously interested? Consider the following. Imagine that you
put nine painters in a room — say Rembrandt, Van Gogh,
Cassatt, Cezanne, Picasso, O'Keeffe, Pollock, Rothko, and
Tamara de Lempicka. You say to them, "Paint an apple or
whatever 'painting an apple' brings to mind." Probably everyone in the room would find the exercise mildly interesting and
would play along (although Van Gogh might storm out — he
was known to flee painting classes). Most would proceed with
only mild enthusiasm, since the task did not originate from them
and probably wouldn't stir them up much. They would be interested enough, but no more interested than if you had asked
them to paint a tomato or an artichoke.

For someone in the room, however, that apple would arouse
uncommon passion and interest. Cezanne famously said, "With
an apple I will astonish Paris!" What he meant was, "Using an
ordinary apple as my starting point, a subject painted a million
times before, I will make some new meaning by virtue of my
artistic vision, my facility with a brush, and my personal response to nature. This apple is exactly the right starting point
for all that!" Eight artists in the room would do some interesting apple work, maybe even some great apple work. But for one
artist, for Cezanne, a productive obsession would flower.

Cezanne decided, in that mysterious way that human beings
decide such things, that an apple would do nicely as the starting point for his productive obsession. He felt something about
the apple; he thought something about the apple; he concluded

something about the apple; something clicked about the apple. Had you presented him with an orange and a banana, he might well have been able to exclaim without a moment's hesitation, "No, sorry, those won't work!" Had you pressed him as to why neither of these perfectly respectable fruits could bear the weight of obsession, he might or might not have been able to provide you with an answer — but in his own mind he would know: oranges and bananas just won't do.

But maybe a cherry or a grape would make him pause. Then he would have to do that thing that each of us must do. He would have to furrow his brow, put his hand to his chin, and think about it. "A grape? How interesting. It is so like an apple in that a million painters have rendered it, and it shines similarly, but, no, it not quite common enough. Anyone can eat an apple; a grape is little bit aristocratic, a little suggestive of nobility. So it won't serve my egalitarian purposes. No, a grape is not an apple! But, ah, what about this cherry? It is certainly beautiful! And it does shine. And while it is more special than an apple, it does not come with the same royal baggage that a grape does. Interesting. I might paint an apple and a cherry side by side! I just might."

How can you decide if the idea you are toying with has arisen from a place of mild interest or one of passionate interest? You might suppose that the answer is something like a question: "Won't a genuine interest grab me in such a way that I can't possibly mistake it for mere interest?" No, unfortunately not, since we know from the history of human effort that it is entirely possible for a person to spend years on a project that seemed rich at first blush and then turned lukewarm. At that moment of choosing, some richer project may have seemed too arduous, too commercially or professionally risky, or too vague to pursue, so a project of lesser interest got selected. A writer, say, convinces herself that she is passionate about her latest idea for a novel: maybe she is and maybe she isn't.

The only sensible course, with respect to each new potential productive obsession that you field, is to pause and think. The thinking I have in mind is not a police interrogation where you shine a bright light into your eyes and keep yourself pinned down until you cry, "Yes, I admit it — this doesn't really interest me!" It's a craftier kind of thinking, in which you go to that remarkable place in yourself where you keep track of your reasons for being. Take the temperature of your interest in that room. Even there, in the room where your reasons for being reside, there are no guarantees that you will guess right about whether this seed of an idea will amaze you and satisfy you once you begin to elaborate it. But it is the best room in the house in which to do the choosing.

Frank, a member of my productive obsession group, proposed the following technique for judging: "It occurred to me to ask myself which possible path, if actively pursued, would yield the greatest disappointment if it didn't work out. Coming at it in this backward way yielded immediate results. Once upon a time I was Johnny Guitar, writing songs and performing in a folk/blues/early-rock vein. Then I just sort of stopped. When I asked my backward passion question, it immediately became clear that I could suck at a *lot* of things and take it in stride, but to finally invest myself in my music and go nowhere? That would be crushing. Bingo. I found where the passion had been hiding!"

Use the one-week mark to clarify the rightness of your productive obsession. For one artist an apple is just an apple; for another it is an explosion waiting to happen. Is your current productive obsession ordinary or explosive?

OBSESSED WITH WILD ORCHIDS

Ask anybody if they love nature and, with only the rare exception, you will get "Of course!" as a reply. Who doesn't enjoy a sunset, a fragrant garden, a great vista? We are built to feel something for nature. Part of our evolutionary makeup inclines us to be moved by blue skies and balmy breezes. But only a much smaller percentage of people are so passionate about nature that it is actually able to generate productive obsessions in them.

The novelist John Fowles was one of these. Nature got under his skin, and wild orchids occupied a special place in his consciousness: "A more special interest I've developed over the years: a bit of a mania for pursuing wild orchids," he explained. "Terrestrial heaven for me is always Crete in late March or early April," the season of orchids. One proof of the power of orchids to obsess him occurred when he found himself hospitalized for a mild stroke at the Royal Free Hospital in London.

Delirious, he began muttering and repeating a weird word: *tenthredinifera, tenthredinifera, tenthredinifera, tenthredinifera*. When he regained his equilibrium and was told of this strange muttering, Fowles explained, "*Ophrys tenthredinifera*, the Sawfly Orchid, is in my opinion the loveliest of all its genus, the Bee Orchids. I had come on a small colony of them in flower only a year before on a mountain in Crete."

Notice what you mutter when you're delirious! There you'll find an obsession or two. You may be paying lip service to some interest — nature, poetry, spirit, travel, philosophy, service, music, collecting — that interests you only about as much as it interests most people, that is, mildly. Take a fearless inventory of these interests and check to see if they amount to genuine passions. If they don't, scoot them off to one side where our everyday interests reside and make some new, precious room for obsession.

chapter seventeen

Two-Week Reports

A T THE END OF THE FIRST TWO WEEKS of your productive obsession program you may find yourself anywhere on the continuum from confused and discouraged to exhilarated and roaring ahead. These first two weeks are bound to produce their share of challenges and also their share of epiphanies. What follows are several two-week reports from participants in my productive obsession group.

Joan explained, "This week I worked hard on a painting that is turning out to be a challenge both technically and emotionally. Each day I've worked on and solved another piece of its puzzle. What's also interesting is that this process of mindfully obsessing has spilled over into my writing. I realized that in order to make my novel as strong as it ought to be I needed to revise more deeply than I'd suspected. My resistance sounded like, 'Where will I find the months to do that?' Now I'm finding a few minutes or a few hours each day to work on the novel — because it's really on my mind. There is such a difference between something really being on your mind and putting it away somewhere! So both the painting and the writing are progressing nicely."

Frank reported, "It's funny how hard it is to obsess about your business while you are actually running it! Every moment of the day is taken up with doing business, which might make it seem like the business is a productive obsession of its own accord, but there is a world of difference between handling business chores and spaciously thinking about what might grow the business or in what direction I ought to take it. All the 'blue sky' thinking that I would love to do gets bumped off the table by everyday demands. So I had an insight — to get away from the business twice a week for long mental lunches where I grab a bite and do some blue sky thinking. It's strange how guilty it makes me feel to steal time away from the business to think about the business! But that's the truth — it does make me feel guilty. So that's what I'm working on, giving myself permission to take a few hours a week to step outside the confines of the business in order to productively obsess about the business."

Phillip wrote, "I chose as my productive obsession a certain problem in cartography and abstract mathematics having to do with fractal geometry and the modeling of bodies of water. It is a real problem but so small that it's hard to assign it the kind of grandness that makes you want to run to it each day. What I really want to do is something as large and grand as taking fractal geometry in some whole new direction, but my mind balks at that bigness, and I keep hearing myself say, 'Solve this problem — that's the obvious task.' So this week has been more a battle than a victory. But I can tell that I'm getting closer to acquiring permission to think big in my field. I may not have won the battle this week, but I may win the war. So my goal is to pay attention to both threads: to the 'small' problem that really does require and deserve my attention and to the 'big' challenges that I want to tackle soon, maybe even as soon as when I get this problem solved."

Stephanie explained, "These two weeks have been good, but it hasn't been all excitement and forward motion. My demons are popping their heads up and trying to derail me. I've been fighting them off, but it's really annoying that they are still so active and such a problem. My biggest stumbling block is still a lack of confidence in my abilities and my capacity to do important things. I've long been aware that I have plenty of fears, and I've vaguely acknowledged them by occasionally talking about them to someone, but I have not done what needs to be done to actually deal with them and move forward. As good as these two weeks have been, they have brought forward this shadow, that I have to figure out what to do about my fears, that I have to not only address them but neutralize them. I can tell that if I don't neutralize them the good obsessing will stop, leaving me high and dry again."

Marcia reported, "I can't say that I'm completely productively obsessing yet, but I'm getting closer. I finished a project I needed to complete in order to have any time at all to think, let alone obsess, and I'm beginning very slowly to gather my thoughts. And then I found myself with an awful cold . . . an excuse? But I did find myself clearing my space, if not obsessively, at least with determination, and that makes a difference. I have a long way to go, but the start I've made is noticeable and energizing. To keep my obsession alive in the face of the realities of living I keep a notebook and journal about it, think about it in the back of my mind, and make time to work on it a priority. I don't think I've come very far, and a lot of this process is like things I've tried before, but I do feel something like a new level of determination."

John wrote, "I chose as my productive obsession to really bite into the screenplay I've been wanting to write about a little-known World War II battle fought in rural France. I've started the screenplay a dozen times, and each time it's felt clichéd and boring. All the scenes leading up to the battle feel like scenes I've seen a million times before. So I gave myself as a prompt, 'Where's the juice?' and I've been obsessing on that question. During the first week I made one false start after another, and then one day during the second week it hit me that the battle itself is the juice. I needed to start right in on the action without any preambles. Not only that, but I knew that if I couldn't write those scenes, there really wasn't any movie. So I bit the bullet and leaped right into the action — and suddenly everything became clear. Right in the middle of the chaos of battle I got perfect clarity about how to design and write the movie. So I am off and running, lost in the forests of France with bombs exploding everywhere."

Vivian explained, "Rather than tapping away in the background of my life like a broken typewriter, my productive obsession is now up-front and personal. I've felt the freedom to let my thoughts run away with themselves and to see where they land, to find the thread and then to lose it, and even to entertain a side obsession. I've tossed out all the previously conceived ideas I had about my project, and now I'm open to all the sparks and nudges, all the odd thoughts and bits of conversations, a sentence here or an image there. I've taken in the wisdom about commitment and come face-to-face with how commitment works, or rather hasn't worked, in my life. I see that not choosing one thing to focus on is only distracting me and preventing me from making real the big picture I envision my life to be. I want to leave all my learned beliefs and their conditioned responses behind and leap into that big picture. What a glorious two weeks this has been!"

Joseph reported, "These two weeks have passed in the blink of an eye. I've hardly gotten myself oriented in the direction of my obsession, let alone really involved with it. I think what I see most clearly is how quickly time passes and how I lose whole years of my time without accomplishing what I'd hoped to. Losing a day here or there would be no tragedy, but to lose so much time is heartbreaking. I need to do something different from just choosing a productive obsession and beginning to let it into my life; I have to completely rethink how I live. I can see why this process is existential, because it brings to the forefront the biggest questions about how a life ought to be lived and about what really matters and what ought to be valued. I can imagine changing a habit — but how do you change a life? Yet nothing less is on the table. I think that my next two weeks will be spent in this uncomfortable existential territory."

Julie explained, "I find myself wasting too much time on stupid activities like Internet surfing. I get frustrated with myself because these stupid activities are obviously an attempt on my part to find meaning somewhere. I constantly have to redirect my attention to my writing, telling myself that the meaning I seek is in the words that I write. My wish is to be able to find meaning in my work and to stop feeling the need to find distractions, as the distractions never provide meaning. It isn't that I've gotten much done these first two weeks, but I have learned something important. Maybe I'm not productively obsessing yet, but I think that what I have done is finally stopped my avoidance tactics and looked squarely at my process. For me, taking this fearless inventory of myself is a prerequisite to productive obsessing."

Amanda wrote, "I realized that I don't get much of anything done if I don't have enough to do; for me more time leads to less work done. So I've started setting up some small projects in addition to writing my novel, putting the materials together close to hand. I like to do embroidery and other fiber arts projects as well as collage work/art journaling and making odd little dolls. I am also learning to play the pennywhistle. So I've put all the materials for these near where I tend to sit and work in the evenings. I'm finding that if I make it easy to fit in little bits of these projects regularly — not every day, but at least a few times a week — I get a lot more done overall. Now that I'm paying attention, I'm finding that a lot of flashes of inspiration come when I let the forefront of my mind focus on something besides my writing. That process, it turns out, helps me stay attuned to my writing."

Bob commented, "I think I'm beginning to see how this is supposed to work. Your obsession starts to become front and center, and your ordinary thoughts begin to recede. I'm noticing that I'm simply not thinking about things that I used to think about, about when a certain ball game might be on, about whether friends might be available for a drink, about whether this is the steak sandwich day at my favorite bistro. My mind has extinguished a zillion nonessential thoughts and keeps returning me to my start-up plan. I've moved entirely from dreaming about my business to starting my business. Nothing about the work is glamorous, and yet it is very satisfying and even grand, this enterprise of paying singular attention to something that I really want to bring into existence. The downside, if it is a downside, is that I am completely spent by 8:00 p.m. and I have to go to bed hours before I used to. But conversely, I've begun to see the dawn, which is quite a masterpiece, and there's nothing like getting in two hours of productive obsessing and compulsive doing before everyone else has even begun stirring."

GOING YOUR OWN WAY

People often discover that in order to pursue their productive obsessions they must go their own way and break from the pack. You start painting like a fiend, you notice that what you're doing looks nothing like the art you've seen recently in galleries, and you stop to ponder: Should you continue and go your own way, or should you rein in your ideas so as to be more marketable? You start researching the chemistry of love, you notice that your results are diametrically opposed to those of the star chemists in the field, you try to publish your results, and you find yourself silenced by the establishment: Should you keep at it, although it feels like banging your head against a stone wall, or should you walk away and research something else? Of course, you may have terrific reasons for deciding not to bang your head against a stone wall; but you should at least muster the internal permission to contemplate that banging.

Consider Luca Turin. Biophysicist, perfume connoisseur, coauthor of *Parfums: Le Guide*, and author of *The*

Secret of Scent, Turin posited a theory of olfactory science that ran counter to commonly held views within the scientific community. Based on his research, Turin concluded that our sense of smell springs from molecular vibrations rather than from the way the shape of molecules match sensors in the human nose. Turin's challenge to olfactory scientists and their strong reluctance to consider his theory is documented in *The Emperor of Scent* by Chandler Burr. In a 2002 review of Burr's book, Turin is painted as "an appealing and genuine maverick who, in bringing quantum mechanics to a physiological problem . . . invited the wrath of academics, not to mention of chemists at the Big 7 producers of artificial scents." Turin's uphill battle to find acceptance for his theories in a world of vested interests may mirror your own battle to find acceptance for your atonal music, technological innovation, teaching method, or surgical approach.

It will take courage and a headstrong attitude to pursue your productive obsession in the face of external opposition. You may know that you are right — and still not have the stomach for the fight. Are you ready to battle for what you believe in?

chapter eighteen

The Turmoil — and Calm — of Process

O UR CHARMING CHARACTERIZATION of productive obsessions as large neuronal gestalts of long duration is just that — a metaphor and not an accurate description of a brain event. A productive obsession is not a single cloud of neurons sitting in the brain for weeks and months on end. There is no large neuronal gestalt hovering in the brain like a blimp over a football stadium. Rather, productive obsessions are profound but indescribable features of what it means to think. What is going on is tremendously more complicated than our simple metaphor, and much more interesting.

Your brain is thinking — about the obsessive idea itself, about how happy it is to be engaged with a productive idea, about the pride it is feeling at venturing the obsession. It is thinking, and it is also thinking about itself thinking. By virtue of engaging with an idea that it finds worthy, it is ramped up, energized, and firing, a state that you'll likely experience as chaotic and tumultuous. By virtue of that same engagement, because it is feeling happy to be working hard and because it is taking pride in its actions, you will also experience a certain calm, the calm of self-satisfaction. Therefore what you are likely to experience is the following: simultaneous turmoil and calmness.

Peggy explained at the two-week mark: "I'm living my productive obsession and experiencing personality growth and change — but not in the way I had expected. Originally I thought that it might be a linear process — or at least a couple of things at a time with a sure plan. Instead, I've been overcome by a new energy — one that is softer and gentler — that urges me forward daily. I do not need to *try*; I just *be*. My colleagues tell me that I look different. I automatically smile. I have a *lot* of energy every day now. I work out or walk almost daily, even in the rain. I can focus on what I want to do. I know my next step, and usually the one after that. I take care of tasks that I don't think I'll enjoy, knowing that in the end I will reach my goal. I am stronger, happier, and very grateful. Piece by piece I'm getting there, and (on most days) I'm loving it. So, yes, I'm churning; but I'm also peaceful."

You will attain this accompanying calmness only if you accept the reality of process. Let's say that you have the gut feeling, based on your years of doing physics and math at a high level, that there is a constant relationship between mass and energy. It is absurd to suppose that there is some seven-step plan or nine-step program that can get you from your gut feeling to "energy equals mass times the square of the speed of light." Yet people are convinced that there is some linear way to write a novel, build a business, or answer a scientific question. Holding to this false hope, when they enter into the turmoil of process

and discover that it is messy, nonlinear, and not what they expected, they quit. If only they could accept that process is exactly this messy, they might grow calm — and enjoy themselves.

There is no way to get from a gut feeling that a constant relationship exists between mass and energy to the naming of that
relationship except by thinking about it, stewing about it, jot-
ting down ideas, testing those ideas, abandoning ideas that
prove wrong, rushing out in the middle of the night to your
computer to check a calculation, and so on. That is, you productively obsess about the relationship between mass and energy
and go wherever the process takes you, whether to a dark room
for deep reflection, a research library for hints and clues, your
wastebasket to discard a day's worth of dead-end calculations,
wherever. If you accept this process, you will experience a special calmness as you try to verify your hunch.

Ralph explained: "For a long time I'd avoided starting my
nonprofit in support of creative tourism because I loathed the
idea of dealing with lawyers, a board of directors, record keeping, and everything else that I knew would come with turning
my dream of helping artists into a down-to-earth, real thing. To
tell the truth, only part of it was fear and loathing; just as large
a part was the simple unwillingness to do the work, to slog
around in starting mode where everything feels like chaos,
confusion, and heavy lifting. I just didn't want to bother.

"Then I accepted the productive obsession challenge, used
the idea of productive obsessing to sell myself on getting into
gear, and got down to the real work of starting. This meant that
I was all over the place, one minute looking for the right 'start
your own nonprofit' book, the next minute trying to discern
what, exactly, I wanted the nonprofit to accomplish, the next
minute soliciting directors before I could even articulate what

their duties would be. Sometimes I felt eight steps ahead of myself, and sometimes I felt eight steps behind. There was nothing like a sense of forward motion; it seemed like everything was in a blender whirring around all at once.

"After a few weeks of this I had a sudden realization. I realized that I was happy. It struck me that it was perfectly possible to have a million things going on in your mind and to still feel calm and centered. When the thing you are doing feels like it has real value and when it makes you proud to be doing exactly what you've always intended to do, then the necessary chaos is just that, necessary and part of the process, and not so hard to live with."

A productive obsession starts with a nugget: a germ of an idea, a hope, a wish for a business, a hunch about some connection between mass and energy, an itch, a dream. Then real process must begin. Real process is the antithesis of phony nine-step programs that make it seem as if you can get from here to there without your idea morphing into something different; without your having to think hard and spend sleepless nights pursuing your thoughts as they hang just out of reach; without your changing your mind about your business model or your palette choice; without, in short, all hell breaking loose in your mind.

But a surprising calmness accompanies all hell breaking loose, an existential calmness that arises because you are genuinely making meaning, following your passions, honoring your interests, and making yourself proud. It is funny that a productive obsession should be both wild and calming, but that is so. No doubt there is a sensible nine-step program for keeping your bathroom tidy, but there is no nine-step program for writing *Crime and Punishment*, curing AIDS, fighting childhood poverty, or composing *Swan Lake*. There is simply no paved road from here to there. There is only the turmoil of genuine process. The amazing news is that despite that turmoil, you will feel calmer and better than if you had skipped trying.

THE GUERRILLA HUNT FOR TYPEFACES

When you engage in genuine process, you have a starting point, but the end point is unknown. You may think that you are writing your novel in the third person, but years later you discover that it must be written in the first person. You may think that your business will focus on herbs, but after six months you discover that spices interest you more. This is the path of genuine process: active engagement in the dark unknown.

Consider how graphic designer Stephan Müller proceeded from a deep love of typefaces to a lucrative business. In her profile of Müller, Hannah Booth writes: "Stephan Müller collects typefaces. He doesn't rip out pages from books or magazines. His methods are more guerrilla, like the time he got down on all fours and did rubbings of foreign car number plates until he had a collection big enough for an entire typeface. Or when, rummaging through a flea market, he chanced upon an Olivetti 'Valentine' typewriter and hit every key until he had a sheet containing each icon." Along with Cornel Windlin he formed the digital font foundry Lineto to distribute his fonts. Lineto.com has since evolved into an international network of designers with addresses in Switzerland, New York, London, Tokyo, Stockholm, Vienna, and Berlin, and they have established a platform for shared attitudes and common interests.

According to artist and blogger Marius Watz, "Lineto and its designers were players who engaged in the spirit of experimentation that dominated graphic design in the 1990s. They challenged typographic conventions with fonts such as Windlin's Moonbase Alpha and championed the new role of the designer as author. Also apparent in projects such as Lego Font Creator, Rubik Maker, and Sign Generator was an understanding of form as system as manifested as software." And the adventure proved lucrative. "Müller was told that his fonts would never sell," writes Booth, "but they became bestsellers with Fontshop. 'They tuned into an emerging zeitgeist for digital-looking type,' he says. 'Luckily, we owned the rights.'"

You start obsessively collecting typefaces because something about them moves you. It is unlikely that you also say to yourself, "This will make me a fortune!" But you continue with your process, collecting more typefaces, finding uses for them, sharing your enthusiasm for them, recognizing their value, creating a website enterprise, and advocating for them in the marketplace. A business is born. Throughout all this a lovely calmness prevails: yes, you are embroiled in the reality of process, but what fun you are having!

chapter nineteen

Three-Week Reports

B Y THE THIRD WEEK of productively obsessing you will have learned a lot about the process. Your initial idea may have morphed a dozen times; you may have completely cycled from the satisfaction of taking your own idea seriously to despair at facing the real work that your idea demands to the satisfaction of accomplishing some of that work. You may have given up on the process and then talked yourself into trying again. A lot is likely to have happened in three weeks. Here are several reports from participants in my productive obsession group.

Janet wrote, "I can't stop thinking about my painting — that's certainly an improvement over my usual way of shoving my ideas out of my mind by saying 'someday.' But overall it's only been a slight improvement, and I'm feeling a little discouraged. So much is going on that the obsession can't really take hold. I have too many classes to teach, and my administrative duties are at an all-time high. Then there's the house to run. It's too much! Almost every day I wish that someone else would make something to eat or clean up my place or deal with the yard so I can get to the studio. I'm often exhausted. I still subscribe to the notion that I have to get my other jobs done before I allow time for my painting obsession — and really, what else can I do? Everything else does require attention. So, I have no idea where I'm headed — but it has to be a different place from this one! At least I know that. Maybe that is enough for now."

Zelda explained, "I found myself putting off posting this check-in. Why? Because three weeks have passed, and I haven't accomplished anything! I spent a lot of time beating myself up and then realized that I was in very familiar territory, the land of 'I've already failed so I might as well give up.' This is a common place for me to reach at week three of anything: writing, exercising, dieting, anything. So instead of putting away my novel I turned to our endurance quotes and talked myself into continuing. I kept my notebooks next to me while I lounged around on Saturday, and by the end of the day I had made a major plot breakthrough. Endurance. Perseverance. They work!

"I'm still disappointed that I'm not further along with my work this close to the end of the month. I don't feel that I'm fully wrapped up in my obsession yet. But I have progress to show, and I have to recognize that this is good. I intend to push further and see just how obsessed I can get."

Albert wrote, "For about a year I'd been distracting myself away from working on my geology dissertation. I put my committee together, got the go-ahead on my topic, completed the research — and then got caught up learning, first Spanish, because I want to do fieldwork in the Andes, and then digital photography, because I want to do a nice job of recording my fieldwork. It was one thing after another.

"I always knew that the dissertation wouldn't take much time if I just did it, but I kept procrastinating. Then this group opportunity came along to call it a 'productive obsession,' and just giving it that name changed everything. I had it virtually done it by the end of the second week, hit a rough spot, felt myself wanting to distract myself with some other activity, but stayed put — and completely finished it in this three-week window. Now all I have to do is defend it — a piece of cake!"

Jeanette explained, "I chose as my productive obsession the question of whether I should start my own practice or stay where I am at the hospital. In the past, I'd bring this subject up to myself and maybe get as far as doing some research on the current ins and outs of private practice — but invariably I'd find the information overwhelming and table the idea. This time something different happened. Because I had this framework of 'productive obsessing' in my mind, the same information that daunted me a few months ago now seemed like emotionally neutral data that I could use to make an informed decision. I would have thought that calling something an obsession would automatically up its emotional ante — but for me, the exact opposite happened. Instead, a new calmness prevailed."

Frank wrote: "By keeping my current sculpture project in mind, and by obsessively considering ways to proceed, I have made real progress — and I have been able to notice when I am pulled off course by distractions. I also noticed how I used to always stop on Friday, as if the universe had put a padlock on weekends and holidays. Holidays and weekends don't mean anything to a productive obsession! So I've begun talking with people who are a part of this project right on through the weekends. The crucial thing I've learned is the distinction between obsession and interest. My sculpture project means so much to me, and by ditching all those mere interests I have opened up huge amounts of time, both for creating the sculpture and for promoting it in the world. Including, now, weekends and holidays!"

Belinda explained, "I've always loved gardening and wondered what it would mean to productively obsess about it. For the first week I had no idea what I was supposed to be thinking about, and I aimlessly read some gardening books. I could tell that I had no idea what I was doing, and the whole process seemed silly and irritating. Why couldn't I just enjoy my garden? Why did I have to go to some extreme place of obsession? The whole idea made no sense to me.

"Then I began to see what the issue was. It had to do with the fact that my love of gardening had shrunk to mere interest and to something smaller than that, to a memory of love, to nostalgia for a time when I actually cared about gardening. The problem wasn't gardening — it was lovelessness. When had I last loved anything? This whole line of thinking caught me up short. I'm not sure you can have a productive obsession if you can't love. So my new productive obsession is to think about where love has gone and how I can get it back. Then the gardening will take care of itself."

Margaret wrote, "Has my productive obsession — to figure out what I can do with the rest of my life to help others — taken hold? Yes, it has! It is so odd, the concept of having permission, but that is what this productive obsession experience has given me. I've been so many times around the block of what to do with my life that at first it felt like the same old place. However, focusing on what I hope to contribute returned me full circle to an obsession I've had my whole adult life with healing children who have been abused. Acknowledging the importance of fully committing to this work has taken me to some deep place and exposed some core conflicts that have kept me from my desired work.

"What I've learned is that when you acknowledge and accept an obsession as valid, you can bring it out into the open where all sorts of new and amazing things can happen. There is a sense of wide openness and focused attention that is working for me for the first time. As I begin to pull the threads of what I've discovered tighter, I can see the fabric forming before my eyes. For this week, I intend to obsess about bringing what I've experienced into a concrete form — a program, a document, something."

Ralph wrote, "I've been on the road for many years, doing as many as a hundred workshops each year, and for all that time I've wanted to put together a new, updated workshop that incorporates what I've learned from delivering my current workshop. But I haven't been able to find the mental space, either on the road or at home between trips, to sit down and think about the new workshop. The very popularity of my current workshop has kept me from making progress on my next workshop!

"So I decided to productively obsess about the new workshop, and here's what I've discovered. I can write on planes, I can write in hotels, I can write anywhere — I just need to call it a productive obsession! The power of naming is flat-out amazing. Nothing in my life has changed, but at the same time everything has changed. At the end of these three weeks I'm already half done outlining the new workshop."

TRAINING BEES TO FEED

In 1912 the German scientist Karl Ritter von Frisch began a lifetime of studying the habits of bees. In the experiments that he and his assistants ran, food was put out for bees at the same time each day, and the bees returned each day at that time to eat. Then the experimenters began skipping feedings, not putting out any food on certain days. Still the bees returned at precisely the same time each day, hoping to be fed.

The researchers discovered the following telling fact. Although the bees could be trained to return regularly within the framework of a twenty-four-hour cycle — that is, at 2:00 p.m. each day or at 4:00 p.m. each day — they could not be trained to return within the framework of some arbitrary cycle. They could not, for instance, be trained to return for feeding every nineteen hours. Something in their physiology demanded that they operate on a twenty-four-hour schedule with circadian regularity.

What does this imply for you? That you have a built-in physiological clock that you can use to train yourself to obsess regularly. Your body has its special relationship to the dawn, to high noon, to afternoon doldrums, to the sun setting, to the night. Use these rhythms in the service of the new habits you're acquiring. Have your obsession rise with the sun; train it to return after dinner for a nightcap and an encore. Marry your productive obsession to your natural rhythms.

chapter twenty

Unproductively Obsessing

FOR YEARS NOW you may have been in the unfortunate habit of unproductively obsessing. Or perhaps the effort to productively obsess has triggered unproductive obsessions. In either case, if your efforts at productively obsessing are being hampered by your unproductive obsessing, you will want to show those unwanted obsessions the door.

How can you tell the difference between a productive obsession and an unproductive one? All the following are typical productive obsessions: chewing on a musical theme day and night until a symphony is born; obsessing about a particular injustice and starting a nonprofit to right that wrong; obsessing about the look of the dawn and getting up early every morning to take digital photographs; obsessing about a software improvement and working late into the night to turn those pressing thoughts into a new program. Without the pressure of a productive obsession to power them, your symphony, non-profit, suite of photographs, or software program might never be born.

An unproductive obsession, by contrast, is a pressing idea that serves no good purpose and that is almost certainly a response to anxiety. You obsess that you haven't locked your front door or shut off the oven, that your hands aren't clean, or that the bridge you're crossing will suddenly collapse. You obsess about your bad luck, your unfriendly co-workers, or your lack of talent. Like a productive obsession, an unproductive obsession is the fruit of mental energy: your mind is whirring. But it is whirring in a worried, fearful way and, in contrast to a productive obsession, generates no energy, provokes no excitement, and does nothing to further your goals and dreams. These are the easy-to-identify but still hard-to-eradicate unproductive obsessions from which countless people suffer.

Sometimes the case is not so clear. Maybe you're intending a certain series of watercolors and you have the sense, which has risen to a conviction and obsession, that the only watercolor paper that will do is XYZ paper that can be found only in the back room of a small Viennese shop that you visited twenty years ago. You spend five days on a fruitless Internet search trying to locate first that little shop in Vienna and then, when that proves impossible, another outlet for XYZ paper. All the while you grow more irritated, agitated, manic, and upset, as your project, in which you've invested so much new meaning, seems to hinge on solving this problem.

Is your hunt for XYZ paper a necessary and unavoidable feature of your productive obsession, or is it an anxiety response to your fear of failing at these new watercolors, a fear you're masking with the bitter complaint, "Without XYZ paper I just can't get started!"? There is no sure answer: sometimes you really do need the equivalent of XYZ paper, and sometimes your obsession with XYZ paper is an unproductive obsession fueled by anxiety. No one knows but you.

Consider one champion of magnificent obsessions, Ludwig van Beethoven. His productive obsessions enabled him to produce beautiful music filled with passion and ideas. His unproductive obsessions, as numerous as his productive ones, caused him and those around him untold misery. Could he not distinguish between the two? Did he even prize his unproductive obsessions, since by obsessing about some perceived slights he could blame the world for his lack of monetary success? What is clear is that he obsessed almost constantly, sometimes in the service of his music and just as often in the service of his paranoia.

Here is a characteristic example of his unproductive obsessing, excerpted from a letter he wrote in which he complained about the liberties taken with his score. You will sense how these complaints go far beyond "standing up for your rights" or "lodging a protest." Each one of his complaints is perhaps fair, justified, and even important. But their sheer number (and I have cut them very short), their vehemence, and the festering mind-set that they represent suggest that we are glimpsing a mind able to turn anything and nothing into an excuse for an unproductive obsession:

> I have just received the *Farewell Sonata*. I see that you have engraved other copies as well with the title in French. Why did you do that? *Farewell* is something quite different from *les adieux*: the first is something which one says only from one's heart, when one is alone, the other something which one says to a whole assembly, to whole cities. Also, you

could have used far fewer plates and this would have facilitated the now so difficult process of reversing, but let this suffice! But how, in heaven's name, does my *Fantasia with Orchestra* come to be dedicated to the King of Bavaria? Kindly answer this question at once. I do not like such things at all. Is it perhaps you yourselves who have affixed this dedication? How does all this hang together? Nor was the *Farewell* dedicated to the Archduke. And why did you not print the date, year, month and day, as I wrote them on my score? You will give me written assurance that in future you will preserve all headings just as I wrote them.

And on and on.

Beethoven's productive obsessions aided him in composing great music, and his unproductive obsessions caused him great pain and contributed to his bitter interpersonal battles and severe depression. Both arose from the same source: a powerful, seething brain that, once it bit into an idea, wouldn't let go. If that something was a folk melody, it gnawed on it for a decade until it found a way to turn it into a sonata or concerto. If that something was a perceived slight, it gnawed on that too, making Beethoven miserable. A mind can go in either direction.

Your personality may support the generation of unproductive obsessions as well as the generation of productive ones. If this is the case, you must pay serious attention to the exact nature of each of your obsessions. Are you focused on a recent negative interaction, a painful memory, a serious worry about the future, or, as so often happens, on many such neuronal drains at once? Are you grand and irascible and obsessing about the world's failure toward you and not on your current meaning investment? Are you so anxious that every effort at productively obsessing leads to an unproductive obsession about why you can't obsess productively? If so, you must pay immediate attention to these significant challenges.

A vast body of literature is aimed at helping you extinguish unproductive obsessions — namely, all the literature on obsessive-compulsive disorder (OCD). If you conclude that unproductive obsessions are a feature of your neuronal landscape, do not exclaim, "The heck with all obsessing!" Work on extinguishing your unproductive obsessions while nurturing your productive ones. Do not throw out the baby with the bathwater.

DIVESTING MEANING

To create a productive obsession, you consciously invest meaning in your budding idea. You not only have an idea, but you also announce that you value your idea and want to pursue it. With unproductive obsessions, exactly the opposite needs to happen. You have an idea — for instance, that you have no talent, that crossing bridges is dangerous, or that your business has no chance of succeeding — and rather than allowing that thought to sit there and infect you, you instantly announce to yourself that you do not value that idea and do not want to pursue it.

You refuse to give your unwanted thoughts credence or significance. You immediately extract or divest meaning from the idea: you strive to quickly reduce its importance and toxicity. That is the key to preventing random negative thoughts from turning into unproductive obsessions. Many people give their random, unwanted negative thoughts much too much credibility. It is not only official OCD sufferers who turn their unwanted thoughts into full-blown unproductive obsessions: millions upon millions of people allow their unwanted, intrusive thoughts too large a place in their minds and in their lives.

How does this happen? As Ian Osborn explains in *Tormenting Thoughts and Secret Rituals*, researchers have demonstrated "that there is an automatic, almost instantaneous, evaluative process lying outside our awareness that assigns different levels of importance ... to intrusive thoughts." Many people have a thought they do not want and, instead of fighting it off, find it credible and even attach a special significance to it. They honor it, and then all mental hell breaks loose. Because they have failed to instantly dispute the unwanted thought, it becomes adhesive; or, to use our previous metaphor, a large neuronal gestalt forms. A random thought about our lack of talent, our lack of luck, or our lack of support turns into an obsession about our lack of talent, our lack of luck, or our lack of support.

You make meaning by actively investing in your productive obsessions. You also make meaning by actively *divesting* meaning from unwanted thoughts that have the power to escalate into unproductive obsessions. One of the features of a brainstorm is the way that you unleash the power of your mind by announcing that you sincerely value your chosen ideas. Demand a similar sincerity with respect to your unwanted, intrusive thoughts. Do not allow them even one ounce of significance.

chapter twenty-one

One-Month Reports

A T THE END OF THEIR FIRST MONTH OF OBSESSING, I asked my productive obsession group two questions to guide their reporting: "What surprised you (either positively or negatively) about trying to productively obsess for a month?" and "What have you learned about productively obsessing that will help you make your second month of productive obsessing more fruitful?" Here are some of their reports.

Jerry explained, "The thing that surprised me the most was how happy I have been this month. Whether the obsession was up front and actively being worked on or streaming in the background while I was doing other things, having the permission to obsess freely really opened me up to intentionally focus on what previously I was trying to do in between the stuff of daily life. It made me realize that I'm the one who makes up the rules that I live by, so it helped me break out of some old rules that weren't mine to begin with. I've felt a sense of free-dom and possibility with that.

"I've learned what a difference it makes in my life when I am giving my attention to something that I love rather than to things that don't matter much. When I do the thing that mat-ters, I am happy and deeply satisfied. The things that don't get done aren't that important in the larger scope of things. And I've learned that giving my attention to my work in this way will lead me where I want to go: toward a business and a life that I am passionate about."

Alice wrote, "What really surprised me is that labeling what I was doing as a productive obsession gave my choice of action more weight, defined it as something important, made me more committed, more interested. It's been my 'job' for the month. Spending time on my art obsession has affected my scheduled drawing time in positive ways. I've been getting to my easel quickly, I've been more inventive in where I'm taking the drawing, and I've wanted to continue beyond the amount of time I'd committed to for the day.

"I'm also recognizing the difference between my negative obsessive thoughts and my productive obsessive thoughts. The negative thoughts just walk circles in my head, and nothing else happens. They are barren ground and depress and weaken me. The productive obsessive thoughts push me into motion. They excite and energize me and they inspire me."

Joel explained, "Just having declared my current project to be 'productive' took the sting out of setbacks and distractions. The simple act of naming something as deeply meaningful has allowed me to return to it many, many times. Surprisingly, the things in my life that I always knew were only 'mere interests' but that took up so much time have regained their rightful place in the background. They still interest me, but I no longer feel guilty when I'm not pursuing them.

"My work involves lots of other people, since we are a group of sculptors engaged in activist art projects located in our community. I noticed that my energy around productive obsessing rubbed off on my fellow artists, and we worked much harder and more quickly this past month, producing our 'carved stone political protest' in half the time we'd anticipated it would take. We enjoyed ourselves, and we made our case in style. Now everyone is looking forward to joining in on a second month of productively obsessing our next creations into being."

Marissa explained, "I was surprised that I could keep obsessing in spite of interruptions and day job busyness. For instance, this week I had a technical problem to solve for a watercolor. I couldn't get in to experiment as much as I wanted, but when I let it go deeply into the simmering creative pot instead of giving up, the solution came to me easily when I did get into the studio. It's like the 'meaning' part of me stays alive now, no matter what. I don't have to lose it whenever life throws in a monkey wrench and then find it all over again. I am definitely going to try my hand at a second month, since I want to get this process firmly under my belt and take my next steps toward making creativity my true life's meaning."

John wrote, "The words *productive obsession* made an impact on me. What surprised me was that I was able to stick to my intention of not whining and not complaining by concentrating on the process of actually obsessing productively. I left the excuses out and concentrated only on the actual daily facts of the 'production side.' It delights me that I am actually seeing the light not so much at the end of the tunnel but all along the tunnel, lighting the way as I go.

"I feel more confident and not as hurried as before, although some of my work is ten years old and needs to get done. It's funny that for years I've felt in a rush to complete this work and despite, or because of, that feeling, I hardly ever worked on it; and now that I am paying real attention and gaining clarity on each specific project, I am no longer rushing and am getting infinitely more done. It used to be about how much I should be getting done — a thought that led to inaction. Now it is all about commitment."

Christopher explained, "I was surprised that by declaring my goal at the start of the month — to get my screenplay finished in thirty days — I was able to return to it easily every day. I had set a self-fulfilling prophecy in motion. Almost best of all, I was able to get to the writing every evening without even thinking about turning on the television — my killer distraction. Not only did I write in the evening, but I found other moments to write: there was a sense of weaving my efforts throughout the month, of keeping my eye on my productive obsession at all times.

"I felt as if my subconscious was working ahead while I was busy with my day job, my new Web-design business. Each time I returned to my screenplay I felt I was already a little deeper than where I left off the last time. It was a strange feeling but also fascinating and exhilarating. The word *productive* was like a magic wand, keeping my obsession an object of pride, something I wanted to return to even after a bad day. It also surprised me how powerful it was to think of my screenplay as 'my work,' as in 'I'm working on my screenplay this evening and can't make it to that movie.' And now a draft is done!"

Charlene wrote, "I'm sitting in my house that hasn't had a

good cleaning in a month. My fridge contains a lot of uneaten food. My desk holds a lot of unopened mail. My laundry basket is overflowing with dirty clothes, and my friends and neighbors haven't seen much of me lately. Oh, that's right ... that's what obsession looks like! Believe me when I say that I'm not boasting. No one is more amazed than I am that I've been obsessed like this. And now that I've had a month to marinate in it I can honestly say that I don't know if being obsessed is good or bad, but I can say for sure that it's not to be missed! I suspect that, like Dorothy, I'll wake up one day and see that I'm back in Kansas, grateful to be home and sad that the journey is over. One thing's for sure: I'll know I've been on one hell of a ride!"

I've been providing readers with a vocabulary of meaning by introducing, describing, and defining phrases such as *making meaning*, *maintaining meaning*, *making meaning investments*, and so on. *Productively obsessing* is a useful addition to this vocabulary of meaning. To add it to your personal vocabulary, spend a month learning about it firsthand.

A MONTH OF EMOTIONS

A month is built into us as part of our biological clock in a way that a week is not. A week is a cultural convention; a month, like a day and like the seasons, has special evolutionary meaning.

The relationship between biological phenomena and the lunar cycle has interested observers for thousands of years. Plutarch noted that the dew was heaviest at the time of a full moon. Cicero and Pliny observed that mollusks varied in size in accordance with lunar rhythms. Aristotle observed the reactions of sea urchins during periods of the full moon so carefully that the sea urchin's chewing apparatus is even today known as Aristotle's lantern.

During this monthly cycle, for men as well as for women, our emotions ride up and down. For example, researchers observing industrial workers concluded that they manifested clear, long-term emotional cycles of approximately four weeks in duration. Factory workers would deteriorate from their normal emotional state to one of apathy and general indifference and at the end of each four-week cycle return to their normal emotional levels. Unless you are keeping very careful track of your emotional peaks and valleys you may have no particular awareness of these trends, but as likely as not you are more "all over the map" than you realize.

Therefore, if you experience some ups and downs during your month of productive obsessing, even if they are significant, consider the possibility that your emotional ride may be only partially caused by your efforts at creating brainstorms. Its main source may be the built-in biological rhythms that affect us every month, regardless of the work we do. We ride up and down naturally and must withstand that emotional roller coaster whether or not we are productively obsessing.

chapter twenty-two

Obsessing in the Middle of Things

H OW CAN YOU PRODUCTIVELY OBSESS in the middle of
things and squeeze your productive obsession into an already jam-packed life? Let's say that you're a junior-college
English teacher trying to obsess into existence a stage play
about a contemporary witch hunt. Your play is set in a court-
room in an unnamed New England town; the defendant is a
young woman charged under an obscure blasphemy law. You
love your premise, although it also scares you, because you wonder if theatergoers will believe that a blasphemy law could still
be on the books in modern-day America. You know that such
laws exist, but will anybody believe you?

Side by side with your productive obsession are your doubts
and fears about the project, among them that you have no idea
how to write a stage play; that people will not accept your
premise; that it will prove impossible to get the play staged; that

if, miraculously, it is staged, no one will come; that if, miraculously, people do come, reviewers will rip your play as a poor imitation of Arthur Miller's *The Crucible*; and so on. All these worries, doubts, and fears keep you from writing very often and make you distractible on those rare occasions when you do get to the writing. You are thinking a lot about your play, but only rarely do you sit down to do any writing.

With papers to grade and lessons to prepare, you are constantly in the middle of your day job, which spills over into every weekend. You are constantly in the middle of your worries about the viability of your play. And, as it happens, you find yourself in the middle of a tense and wearing conflict with your mate about finances, parenting, and the very viability of your marriage. You are in the middle of so much that it is no wonder that your productive obsession amounts to an inconsistent thing. You do love your play; you would love to obsess about it, if only you had the time and the emotional equilibrium; but as it now stands your play has another zip code.

Most people harbor the hope that "when things change" or "when things improve" they will do a better job of productively obsessing and paying attention to their brainstorms. It is much smarter not to wait for that mythical time to arrive. Even if circumstances changed for our teacher — let's call her Mary — and she found herself with a less busy semester, her academic duties would still eat up days on end, and she would still be confronted by her doubts about the play, her domestic issues, and so on. If her domestic issues miraculously improved, she'd still be confronted by stacks of essays to read and by her lack of confidence. If she gained some needed confidence, the papers and the problems with her husband would remain. Even if *everything* changed, there would still be the unavoidable difficulty of birthing a play and making it good and strong. In short, waiting is not the answer — it never is.

How might Mary proceed to productively obsess in the middle of her tense, busy life? First, she must believe that her play matters. Doubting that it matters will destroy the large neuronal gestalts she is trying to cultivate as surely as a bony finger punctures a soap bubble. If the only way she can convince herself that her play matters is to announce every hour on the hour, "My play matters!" that is what she must do. She must also reduce the importance of that stack of ungraded papers, that angry interchange with her husband, and that worry about the believability of her play's premise. If her doubt about her play's basic premise rises to an annoying 7 or 8, with 1 being a virtual absence of worry and 10 being sheer panic, she needs to exclaim to herself, "Enough with that worry! It just doesn't serve me!"

She must deeply learn the idea of investing meaning in the increments of time available to her. If she has an hour between classes, that hour will slip away unless she gets in the habit of saying, "This hour is too valuable to waste! I'll work on my play for fifty minutes and then clear my head for ten." Or, alternatively, she might say, "As much as I can't stand the idea of grading papers at this moment, I'll use this hour to grade so that I'm free to work on my play when I get home." That is, she might invest meaning in tackling her play, or she might invest meaning in tackling her grading for the sake of her play. Whether she works on her play or grades papers, she will have turned that easily lost hour into an hour of intentional meaning.

For your second month of productively obsessing, as you recommit to this process and this practice, keep these points in mind. Announce that your productive obsession really matters.

Act on it whenever you have a chance, in whatever increments of time are available to you, even if those increments are ten minutes here and fifteen there. Consciously reduce your neuronal involvement with those things that matter less — those stacks of papers, those stray doubts about the smartness of your project — and consciously increase your neuronal involvement with your productive obsession.

Life is more than a series of productive obsessions. It is also a kiss here and a hug there, a round of laundry and a bit of dusting, this small crisis and that small blessing. But at its very heart life may indeed be measured by the productive obsessions we name and nurture, since each one represents a serious love and a powerful existential commitment. Take this second month as an opportunity to strengthen your connection to your productive obsession and deepen your understanding of the process of productive obsessing.

PAUSING FOR LOVED ONES

You want to do a superb job of attending to your productive obsessions. But you also want to do a superb job of living the rest of your life. It is less than honorable to drop everything important to pursue your passions, especially if what you are dropping are your loved ones.

Roger Tory Peterson, renowned ornithologist and naturalist, forever changed the way people react to, and interact with, nature. His initial *Field Guide to the Birds*, published in 1934, introduced amateur naturalists to the life of birds, providing anyone curious enough to pause and look with the information necessary to identify the vast variety of birds in their midst. His obsession — beginning when birds "took over" his life in the seventh grade after an experience with a Northern flicker awakened him to "the world in which we live" — caused him to spend the rest of his life cataloging birds.

Often Peterson would work around the clock with an intensity that kept him isolated from his wife and two sons, even when he was physically nearby. It seems, however, that his family adapted to his work rhythms and recognized his work as being of paramount importance. Even though Peterson's energy for his work was intense and all consuming, his son Lee recalls that "not once, when I would bring him a bird's nest, an insect, or something else to be identified, do I remember him not pausing in what he was doing and focusing on answering my questions." On the other hand, Lee also described his father as someone "just passing through" rather than part of the household. Did Peterson's obsession come at too high an interpersonal price, or did he pause long enough for the human beings in his life?

You need to cultivate productive obsessions because they are enriching and meaningful. But don't ignore the rest of life or your interpersonal obligations. There is no higher path than productively obsessing *and* being present for your loved ones.

chapter twenty-three

Journeys and Not Destinations

W E LIVE EMBROILED IN PROCESS. Yet when we step back and try to think about the history of our mind at work we tend to focus on destinations. We look at a portfolio of the drawings that we've done, and we see them as objects and not journeys. We consider a personal problem that we solved, and we focus on its solution, not on the twisting path that got us to that solution. Life becomes about numbers — our two divorces, the fifty countries we've visited, the ten jobs we've held — and not about the experience we had on the eightieth day of writing our novel, when its plot shifted, or the slow process we went through getting our business off the ground.

In our journals we may find the record of our ongoing process, but as we reflect we consolidate all those processes into round numbers. This is the natural way that we catalog our experiences. The roundness of those numbers, however, causes us to forget exactly how twisting each path is, how often our smart thinking gets dull and our obsessing turns sour, and to what extent we experience a lifetime of emotional ups and downs and intellectual ins and outs in a single hour.

Remembering that we are on a mapless journey, how often our mind wanders, and how many detours appear on our path reminds us that we can slip from productively obsessing into unproductively obsessing in the blink of an eye. You've been productively obsessing your business into existence, your confidence slips for a moment, and suddenly you find yourself obsessing about whether you made the best choice on your logo colors or got the lowest price on your office furniture. You are still obsessing about your business, but because of some internal shift your obsession became unproductive. Remembering that this is likely to happen will help you notice when it does.

These shifts can occur in amazingly subtle ways, moving us micron by micron away from productivity to worry and causing new neuronal gestalts to form in the service of complete detours. We are still thinking; our mind is still whirring; but our thoughts are off-key. Anything can cause these shifts: a week of cloudy weather, an existential wonder, or, as in the following report, watching reruns of *The Sopranos*.

Lisa explained, "These last weeks it hasn't been that fruitful or as easy to productively obsess. I've found myself sitting down to do some work and my mind suddenly goes blank or darts around excitedly looking for the nearest exit. One thing that changed is that I began watching reruns of *The Sopranos* with my boyfriend, who has never seen the show. The therapy episodes and the relationship dynamics were interesting to me in the beginning. Since the work I do involves women's empowerment, thinking about the portrayal of women on *The Sopranos* made some sense. But now I wonder.

"The show's portrayal of women began to spin ever so subtly in the background of my mind; and then it began to consume me. It became clear that this was taking the place of my productive obsession. Those depictions gave me a clear picture of some issues that need addressing in my own life, so in one sense it wasn't completely unproductive. But in another way it was, since my brain is not obsessing on my own work and instead is creating anxiety and frustration. I need to do my own work now!"

Each of us takes these sorts of detours at one time or another. For example, in the course of writing this book I began to wonder if I should nominate Beethoven as the poster boy for the subject of productive obsessions, just as I had nominated Vincent van Gogh as the poster boy for my book on existential depression. Beethoven was an example par excellence of someone blessed with productive obsessions and burdened by unproductive ones; and unlike many composers, Mozart among them, Beethoven often chewed on musical ideas for decades at a time, a phenomenon that I thought would be interesting to tie into the idea of the persistence of certain large neuronal gestalts. Couldn't the book sensibly focus on him?

That question began to dominate my thoughts. This book morphed into something called *Beethoven's Brain*, and I began to pore over Beethoven's letters and a host of related material. The idea of focusing on Beethoven made sense — and yet I suspected that I was off on a tangent. Was I following the right path or heading down a dead-end alley? You can't snap your fingers and demand an answer to such questions. I had to put the book aside and give my brain a rest. When, months later, I returned to it, I knew that it would be a mistake to focus on Beethoven.

I didn't need to fill up pages with his tantrums and irritations, and I didn't need to fill up pages with paeans to his music. Beethoven belonged, but not on center stage.

As you journey down your path, detours will open up. Some will arise because you've had a genuinely interesting idea that you must process to see if it should be paid real attention. Say that you're building the website for your business. It will have a membership option, and you're researching which membership program to purchase. Suddenly you start obsessing about alternatives to the membership model. Did you make the switch because it became too taxing to think about membership options, because the high cost of the one that you like best is making you anxious, or because a smart alternative to the membership model is percolating in your brain?

At such times your best bet is to stop everything, take a long moment, and clear your head. Often all that is needed is a small but genuine break. It's entirely likely that the answer will come clear if you can quiet your mind and let your neurons sigh and relax. They'll know how to gather again and resume thinking; and they'll thank you by working harder and thinking better once that break is over. We are asking our roiling brain to monitor itself and reckon whether it's on track. It can do exactly that, but sometimes it will need a nap or a splash of cold water. Other times it may need a few days' break. Occasionally it may need a respite lasting weeks or even months. The principle to apply is the following: start with a small break, and only then move on to a day away or a weekend vacation, and in this incremental way proceed to weeklong or monthlong respites.

Whether or not you reach a satisfactory destination with your current productive obsession, know that you've been on a journey that required your full attention and that tested your mettle.

Sometimes a satisfactory destination will elude you: your research will hit a dead end; your business won't launch; the everyday problem you had hoped to solve will remain perplexing. Other times you will hit pay dirt. Even then, that pay dirt will prove a transitory marker between fascinating journeys. The book you wrote will appear on your shelf, but your mind will already be racing down the rails in pursuit of its next obsession.

PASSIONATE BREAKS OF SHORT DURATION

Maybe you've been working on your productive obsession for many hours straight and have grown exhausted. Maybe you've been working on it for only a little while but have hit a snag. When you feel stuck and sense that you're inclined to take an extended break — which may signal that you secretly want to throw in the towel — try to opt for a break of short duration instead. That may be all you really need. Take a brisk walk around the block; make a cup of tea; or, as many artists and writers learn to do to deal with hours of total concentration, take a brief nap.

In *Writers Dreaming*, novelist Charles Johnson explains in an interview with Naomi Epel: "I knew that chapter three [of *Middle Passage*] needed something. . . . I have this tendency to write until I'm just exhausted and then go and take a nap or something. So I did that. . . . As soon as my head hit the pillow I started to drift off . . . and I saw this image." The image ultimately yielded the scene that fleshed out chapter three. "I knew the book needed something," Johnson continues, "but it wasn't until I sort of halfway went to sleep that something popped up in my mind."

Johnson's intention is crucial: he knows that he needs a break but a break in the service of his obsession. He isn't meaning to abandon the book or skirt this particular plot challenge. Rather, he is passionately interested in solving the book's current problem, and his brain knows it. It takes a nice little break, providing Johnson with some mental rest; but even as it rests it continues working out of conscious awareness, solving the problem it has been given.

When you want to take a break from your productive obsession, because it's exhausting you, because some problem has arisen that needs a little time and distance, or because, well, you just need to, try to make the break a short one — and while you're on break continue holding your productive obsession in a corner of awareness. It won't burden you there, and by keeping it close you continue working on it and need not fear losing it.

chapter twenty-four

Productive Obsessions
and Critical Thinking

WHY DO OUR SCHOOLS NOT TEACH CRITICAL THINKING?
Educators agree that teaching critical thinking skills is
education's number one priority. Yet classroom observers report
that in over 95 percent of the classrooms they visit, no critical
thinking skills are taught. Students are forced to memorize and
repeat. Parents ask, "What did you learn today?" and not
"What have you been thinking about?" When some thinking
does occur at school, it happens only inadvertently. You would
think that our society would want its schools to prepare young
people to think critically, make meaning, demand freedom, and
bravely face the facts of existence. Yet our schools function primarily as custodial warehouses and temples to memorization.
What happened?

These aren't idle questions meant to detour us from our subject. Your current ability to productively obsess is directly and

intimately related to your childhood experiences, and little in your childhood helped you to master critical thinking or productive obsessing. With only the rare exception — exceptions that help turn certain children into our best and our brightest adults — children are discouraged from critically thinking and productively obsessing by the four institutions that shape them: family, school, peers, and society. If you are having trouble today choosing and nurturing productive obsessions, your childhood experiences are largely to blame. You never learned to productively obsess at school, at home, among your friends, or in any of our cultural institutions. That explains a lot.

Why should this be the case? Why is critical thinking lauded in theory and avoided in practice? The simple answer is that many adults prefer that their children not do much thinking. They want their children to get good grades, obey, fit in, find a job, play sports, salute the flag, and kneel in prayer — really, anything but think. They portray thinking as effete and even as dangerous. Adults who think this way and act this way are endeavoring to preserve their privileges and do not want young people asking difficult questions, disputing their authority, or threatening them with exposure. Self-interest makes too many adults secretly wish that schools would do little more than mind their kids and prepare them for work.

Our education system listens to the wishes of these many adults. An unspoken agreement is reached by all involved — parents, politicians, school board members, school superintendents, principals, teachers and, with that army of adults aligned against them, students themselves — that thinking is dangerous and should not be countenanced. Therefore "learning" is supported, and "thinking" is discouraged. Nobody's feathers are ruffled if you provide your students with another plane geometry theorem or twenty more French vocabulary words. The system is set up to support exactly this sort of transaction. There is a subject called plane geometry, there is a teacher who teaches plane geometry, there is a student who learns plane geometry and who is tested in plane geometry, there are uses for plane geometry, both as a pillar in a liberal education and as a stepping stone to solid geometry, and this all makes perfect sense. Doesn't it?

No, it doesn't. The tyranny of subject matter, with one subject following another from kindergarten to graduate school, leaves little or no time for critical thinking or productive obsessing. The full-scale solution to this problem would be to reduce to a minimum the teaching of traditional subjects and to completely revamp how we think about educating our children, focusing on a "thinking" model rather than a "learning" model. Since this full-scale solution is certainly out of reach — primarily because adult society doesn't want its authority questioned by thoughtful children — a smaller, perhaps more obtainable solution is the following: to have an hour or two each school day, from elementary school through graduate school, devoted to thinking.

Somebody with a new name might lead this portion of the day: not a "teacher" but a "critical thinking coach" or a "critical thinking facilitator." This person could, of course, be a traditional teacher, but for this hour or two she would coach and coax rather than teach and test. What might occur during this two-hour block? Students would actually learn critical thinking skills and the power of productive obsessions. The device employed to help them learn these critical thinking skills would be the "big question" — that is, something genuinely interesting. They would be assured right off the bat not only that there are probably no easy answers to the problem but also that the problem might not actually be solvable. They would be given all possible permission not to worry about rightness and to focus on using their brain and engaging their imagination.

When a student tried to solve a given problem with a slogan-size, too-easy answer, it would be the critical thinking coach's job to say, "But what if. . . ?" helping the student, and the whole class, to realize what a poor job slogan-size answers do in addressing human-size problems. For instance, if the "big question" was, "In what circumstances would you turn a friend in to the police?" and a student replied, "As a matter of principle, I never turn friends in!" the critical thinking coach would continue ever so mildly, "What if your friend was engaged in a plot to kill your family?" If during a "How do you know if someone is crazy and should be put in an institution?" discussion a student offered up, "They're crazy if they look crazy!" the critical thinking coach might respond, "So if an actor on stage were looking crazy, you would lock him up?" The students would be forced to think.

Some of these big questions might be the following: How do you know when you're addicted to something? How do you decide if you should or shouldn't support a war your country is engaged in? How do you decide if space exploration is or isn't an important societal goal? If species naturally go extinct, what is the rationale for preserving biodiversity? Under what circumstances is it ethical to lie? Which should a society strive to uphold: the freedom to accumulate wealth or the fair distribution of wealth? What is "personality"? If young people are introduced to questions of this size and scope, they will have no trouble productively obsessing as adults.

It should be clear that these are questions not even "the

experts" can answer and, likewise, that these are infinitely more provocative and mind-expanding questions than "What was the date of the Battle of Gettysburg?" or "Into what genre does *Wuthering Heights* fall?" Of course our new breed of critical thinking coach will have to remain on her toes as she facilitates these class discussions: she'll need to anticipate the kinds of slogan-size answers that students are likely to give and be ready to help them see the paucity of such answers. These new coaches would help students embrace complexity, demand context, appreciate the subjectivity of evaluation, form and test hypotheses, change their mind based on new evidence, grow comfortable with not knowing, and think big. Can you imagine a better preparation for a lifetime of productive obsessing than wrestling with such questions in school?

Since every educator pays at least lip service to the idea that critical thinking is an admirable educational goal, it might be possible to nudge at least some school districts and some schools in the direction of revising the school day to include, in addition to subject matter classes, "critical thinking modules." This is our best hope to get our youth thinking, since they are unlikely to be encouraged to think at home, where many parents want only obedience; or with their peers, where the major dynamics are about acceptance; or anywhere else in the culture — not while watching television, not while sitting in church, not while playing a video game, not while cheering at a ball game. School is our best chance. Maybe a small revolution will occur, and classrooms will become more thoughtful places.

It's possible that you can't keep a good productive obsession down — but everything about mainstream education is geared to do just that. So it is no wonder that you may have some problems embracing your own big ideas. When you want to throw up your hands and cry, "Productive obsessing is not for me!" remember how infrequently you were invited to think hard as a child. Probably your brain is still filled with the sorts of random facts that serve you in trivia games and nowhere else — with more such random facts infiltrating all the time from our media avalanche. Let go of your ability to recite our fifty state capitals. That was the sort of thing they wanted you to know in childhood, to keep you from having grown-up thoughts. Now is the time for mature thinking.

YOUR NOBSON NEWTOWN

Did pondering your early education flood you with memories of sharp pencils and small desks? One man brought his fascinating obsession to life with those very childhood pencils. Paul Noble is best known for his pencil-and-paper drawings of an imaginary town he invented: one "Nobson Newtown." Noble's Nobson Newtown drawings fill enormous panels and depict life devoid of humans. Weaving both obvious and oblique references to history and literature into his bizarre world dominated by images of decay, Noble has constructed a vivid social commentary with everyday graphite.

Noble's intention is to shock us, confound us, terrify us, and make us think. The familiar and the friendly are turned into telling horrors. As Richard Cork explains in the *New Statesman*: "Fish, birds and furry little beasts abound. Yet any pleasure proves short-lived, because hypodermic needles can also be seen, injecting the creatures with substances that render them helpless. They lie prone in cages, waiting to be subjected to all kinds of unimaginable experiments." Who knows what child in third grade is right now creating her private Nobson Newtown while her teacher is going on about Columbus! Our obsessions start when we're young — and all that's required is a pencil and piece of paper.

Nobson Newtown is one version of critical thinking. There are countless other versions available to you: the critical thinking of scientific research, the critical thinking of musical composition, the critical thinking of cultural commentary, the critical thinking of personal problem solving. School did not support you in becoming an excellent critical thinker — simply too much emphasis was placed on dates, places, and the naming of things. Maybe you sat there chewing on your pencil, bored to death. Now is your grown-up chance to think!

chapter twenty-five

The Persistence of
Productive Obsessions

IF WE BETTER UNDERSTOOD MEMORY AND IMAGINATION we might discover that memory is in part the way that persistent productive obsessions recombine instantly and that imagination is our repertoire of persistent productive obsessions dynamically recombining. Sometimes we get information, like the look of a certain date tree in an oasis garden or the look of a certain patch of the moon's surface, from memory. Sometimes we engage our imagination and receive new information, like the look of a date tree in a moon garden. Both memory and imagination are surely repositories for, and composed of, thoughts that have risen to the level of obsession that we have chosen to or can't help but save.

Certain productive obsessions are bound to thread their way through your life, appearing here as a theme in the novel you write, there as the destination for a family vacation, and somewhere else as membership in a group or as an impulsive purchase. Say you're obsessed with the idea of justice, as productive an obsession as our species can entertain. That obsession might provoke you to write a screenplay about an obscure abolitionist, visit Revolutionary landmarks, join the ACLU, and buy George Orwell's collected writings. These results are only the tip of the iceberg: if justice is always on your mind, as it would be if it rose to the level of a persistent productive obsession, then your whole life would be filtered through that lens, as would your memory and your imagination.

Throughout this book we've been discussing the idea that a productive obsession is something that you choose, bite into, pursue, and eventually put to bed as it runs its course. Your novel is written and published; you move on to your next novel. You build your current business and eventually sell it; you move on to your next business. A math problem consumes you; you solve it or give up trying to solve it and move on to your next challenge. In each of these cases the process is intricate, and although the journey is circuitous, there's nevertheless a linear quality to it and a sense of serial replacement. One productive obsession follows another as each spent obsession dissipates and those previously occupied neurons loosen their grip.

Here we're looking at a different idea, at the notion that some percentage of our obsessions, because they continue to interest us and continue to serve us over time, remains available in memory and imagination. They are always available to us because we've trained our neurons to send us certain imagery as we soon as we begin our new poem or a certain beat as we compose our march. This repertoire of intentional memories sits in the wings, and appropriate memories leap forward as needed. Without the cultivation of these persistent productive obsessions, we might not even possess that thing we call vivid imagination.

Say, for example, that something about the torrid heat of your Algerian childhood becomes a complicated remembrance. That heat begins to stand for the heated conflict between your French compatriots and the native Algerian Arabs among whom you lived and becomes associated with the accidental nature of birthplace and turns into a symbol of alienation and absurdity. This is Albert Camus's story. The Algerian heat threads its way through his novels, pressuring the protagonist in *The Stranger* to kill an Arab, provoking a barber in *The First Man* to slit the throat of a customer, and making itself felt by its absence in *The Fall*, a novel set in a murky Amsterdam. That heat obsessed him, acquired various layered meanings, and entered his lexicon of symbols and metaphors. Just as a snowflake was more than a snowflake to the Snowflake Man, the heat of Algeria was more than mere heat for Camus.

Why do persistent productive obsessions of this sort form in the first place? Freud had one idea: the idea of creativity as sublimation. He argued that human beings employ creativity as a defense against acting on their dangerous impulses. You love fire and have a deep craving to set something on fire; that is your id speaking. Your superego steps in and demands that instead of setting anything on fire you create paintings ablaze with reds and oranges. You want to steal your neighbor's husband: instead you write a romance in which your heroine does that stealing. You're furious at your father: instead of killing him you write an opera in which a father is brutally murdered. Freud argued that human beings evolved with this mechanism for defusing unwanted urges and, as a lucky by-product, art got created.

We can think about this a bit differently. Rather than picturing this process of turning unproductive thoughts into productive ones as sublimation and as purely defensive, we can conceptualize it as a conscious, transformative process in which we knowingly turn unproductive obsessions into productive ones. Rather than unproductively obsessing about stealing our neighbor's husband, we quite consciously and productively obsess a novel into existence, one that includes a theft of that sort. Here the transaction is more conscious and transparent and, to use Freud's language, less a tug-of-war between id and superego and more a decision made by the ego. You experience some powerful impulse — let's say, a sexual one — and you consciously announce, "No, this isn't going to seduce me into an affair; this is going right into my next suite of paintings!"

A second reason that persistent productive obsessions form, in addition to appearing as reactions to our powerful primitive impulses, is that our loves abide over time. We do not love a certain blue shade, a certain high note, or the fact that parallel lines never meet only now; if we really love them, then we love them forever. We love what we love indefinitely, and the neuronal translation of abiding love is a repertoire of persistent productive obsessions that reside in memory and are available to our imagination. In other words, we store what we love.

Probably both motives are at play much of the time. An artist struggles with some impulse or urge and takes that struggle into his art, where he attempts to defuse it. He would love to set actual fires but instead introduces fire imagery into his plays and has his characters burn with desire and the neighborhood church or brothel burn to the ground. At the same time, that fire imagery holds a whole constellation of meanings for the artist and becomes something that he loves independently. Real fires may or may not interest him any longer, but fire imagery becomes a persistent productive obsession that he can use — as lit candle, as burning bush, as conflagration — in the art he creates.

Tennessee Williams provides us with a perfect example of this process. Williams always had fire imagery ready and waiting. It obsessed him and played a significant role in virtually all his plays. It stood for no one thing, since sometimes it represented a burning creative fire, sometimes it stood for sexual desire, sometimes it operated as a mechanism for purification, sometimes it served as the way to atonement. Fireworks, fire escapes, smoldering cigarettes, burning buildings, self-immolation: some bit of fire is always showing up in Williams's imagination. Just think of how *The Glass Menagerie* opens: with a fire escape, "a structure whose name is a touch of accidental poetic truth, for all of these huge buildings are always burning with the slow and implacable fires of human desperation."

Or take his play *Summer and Smoke*. That play begins with a fireworks display attended by the main characters, among them Alma, the unmarried daughter of a minister, and John, a young doctor who has recently treated "fifteen kids for burns," burns presumably brought about because the children had been playing with firecrackers. Unbeknownst to Alma, John tosses a firecracker at her, a firecracker that causes her to "spring up with a shocked cry" and exclaim, "There ought to be an ordinance passed in this town forbidding firecrackers." With the lighting of a last spectacular firecracker, a Roman candle with seven puffs of light, the opening scene ends as Alma attempts to engage John in conversation. As she makes this effort, John nervously lights and extinguishes one cigarette after another.

What does this idea of persistent productive obsessions

mean for you? First, if you want to become more imaginative, cultivate productive obsessions. Second, if you want to improve your memory, cultivate productive obsessions. Third, if you want to store your loves — those summer evenings from childhood, that Chinese red you saw last winter, those sculptural shapes you encountered in a park in Oslo — cultivate productive obsessions. Some number of your cultivated productive obsessions will persist in memory and imagination. If you want to add an obsession with free speech to your love affair with justice or an obsession with Mars's two moons to your repertoire of painting icons, practice the habit of cultivating productive obsessions. Your memory and your imagination will thank you.

AN OBSESSION WITH FIRE IMAGERY

Here are some of the many uses to which Tennessee Williams put his persistent productive obsession with fire imagery:

Maggie in *Cat on a Hot Tin Roof*: "When something is festering in your memory or your imagination, laws of silence don't work, it's just like shutting a door and locking it on a house on fire in hope of forgetting that the house is burning. But not facing a fire doesn't put it out."

Tom in *The Glass Menagerie*: "Oh, Laura, Laura, I tried to leave you behind me, but I am more faithful than I intended to be! I reach for a cigarette, I cross the street, I run into the movies or a bar, I buy a drink, I speak to the nearest stranger — anything that can blow your candles out! For nowadays the world is lit by lightning! Blow out your candles, Laura — and so goodbye."

Interchange in *A Streetcar Named Desire*:

BLANCHE: Marry me, Mitch.

MITCH: I don't think I want to marry you any more.

BLANCHE: No?

MITCH: You're not clean enough to bring in the house with my mother.

BLANCHE: Go away, then. Get out of here quick before I start screaming fire! Fire! Fire! Fire!

Interchange in *Battle of Angels*:

VAL: The place next door burnt down.

MYRA: What's that got to do with it?

VAL: I don't like fire. I dreamed about it three nights straight so I quit. I was burnt as a kid and ever since then it's been something I can't forget.

The same can be said for Tennessee Williams. His obsession with fire imagery is one that never leaves him. From the beginning of his writing career to the end, Williams turned first to fire whenever he needed an image.

chapter twenty-six

Turning Your Productive Obsession Off

THERE ARE PSYCHOLOGICAL, PRACTICAL, AND ETHICAL reasons for demanding of yourself that you turn off your
productive obsession. Your goal isn't to rev yourself up into
a clinical mania, forget to pay the rent, cavalierly ignore your
loved ones, or drive other good thoughts out of your brain. Productive obsessions allow us to make meaning, but we don't put
them on a higher pedestal than that, we don't give up everything
in their favor, and we don't allow them to lead us about by the
neurons. When the time comes for a productive obsession to be
shut down for the day, it is your job to open the valve and let the
steam escape.

You ramped up your productive obsession in order to make
meaning: you made the calculation that your large sculpture,
grand opera, worthy nonprofit, or scientific research mattered
to you. Having made that calculation, your secret worry may be

that if you are not engaged with your project your life will feel dull, barren, and pointless. It's very hard to stop painting if you harbor the fear that life will feel meaningless as soon as you put down your paintbrush. This fear needs addressing. Once you realize that you are capable of making meaning in multiple ways, the powerful existential need to maintain your productive obsession lessens and you regain control of your mind.

Most people remain stuck in first gear, unable to ramp up their productive obsessions. A smaller percentage of people, often the most imaginative and productive, find themselves afflicted with the opposite problem, that they can't turn off their productive obsessions. Though their numbers may be smaller, they are likely to suffer significantly from their inability to cease obsessing. Picasso claimed that he was incapable of passing a blank canvas without feeling the urgent need to fill it up. The results of this poignant affliction were a huge body of work and a persistent unavailability that provoked interpersonal disasters. You may produce fewer paintings or novels if you get in the habit of controlling your obsessions, but what you lose in inventory you gain in mental health.

Your productive obsession must not become the one and only place where you make meaning. You get to decide what is meaningful to you, and you mustn't decide that your productive obsession is so meaningful to you that you will refuse to tolerate any interruptions, even from your child when she wants to share a story. If you make that decision, you will be making a grave mistake. You want to decide that your productive obsessions, as meaningful as they are, are nevertheless only one of the ways that you meet your existential needs. You can meet them by learning how to "just be"; you can meet them by relating and loving; you can meet them in a score of ways that are each as rich as obsessing. Once you have this repertoire in place, you are in the position to turn your obsession off as appropriate and enjoy another place of meaning.

Right at this moment maybe nothing feels as meaningful as your obsession. Maybe you have no love life, no passions apart from your obsession, and only worries and loneliness waiting in the wings. What, for instance, if an addiction is waiting? Given the likelihood that a person who is "good" at obsessing may also be "good" at getting addicted, isn't such a person wise to keep obsessing? It turns out that controlling a productive obsession is a complicated affair: you need existential readiness to make meaning in supplemental ways, an ability to deal with the anxiety that surfaces as soon as you stop obsessing, an in-place recovery program for any addiction issues that dog you, and more. It is much harder to turn off a productive obsession if, in the silence that follows, all hell breaks loose — the hell of loneliness, the hell of the bottle, the hell of meaninglessness.

Frank, a physicist, explained it this way: "I'm involved in the world of string theory. Part of me is fascinated by my research and my speculations, and part of me is attached to the research because I hate going home at night to my empty apartment. So I stay at the lab as late as I possibly can. I can tell that sometimes I would love to stop obsessing and just have a meal with somebody or take in a movie or do something normal, but it's harder to contrive a normal evening than it is to keep obsessing. For me to control my productive obsession with string theory I would have to create a life first — and that feels like a taller order than figuring out the ultimate nature of the universe."

Sara wrote, "I run an Internet-based business from a room at the back of our house. I never want to leave that room.

Partly that's because the details of the business are endless —
every other minute another email arrives requiring attention.
But that's only part of it. My husband doesn't work and hasn't
worked for years. That means that he's always around. It isn't
that he's moping around; he's usually tackling some project or
doing something useful. But I actually can't stand seeing him not
contributing and not honoring an it-ought-to-go-without-
saying agreement that he do his share. So I'm trapped back
there, obsessing about the business in part because I want to
be and in part because I'm in hiding. I'm convinced that if he
were out of the house working, I'd be able to shut down my
business obsession and relax."

Mark confessed, "I know that my obsession with noir
movies is only partly healthy. The database that I'm creating will
be useful to researchers, and I've gotten tons of appreciation for
the work I've done collecting and cataloging information. And
I love the genre — I genuinely love it. Put me in front of a noir
movie, even a terrible one, and I'm happy. But I also know that
my fascination with these black-and-white movies and that
long-gone world has to do with nostalgia and my reluctance to
make sense of the here and now, which seems overwhelming and
terrifying. If I found it easier to be in this century I'd spend less
time in the last, but as it is I'd rather dissect a haunting jazz score
than deal with reality."

What will help you manage your productive obsessions?
Having a good, rich life in place. You want to know that when
you leave your productive obsession it isn't for a second-rate experience. You need to have something to turn to in order to turn
away from your productive obsession. You want your productive obsession to feel rich, and you want the rest of life to feel
rich also.

LEARNING TO FORGET

Researchers who study obsessive-compulsive disorder wonder if part of the problem is that sufferers have "trouble forgetting." If you tell two people that the sun is destined to burn out in 7.5 billion years, a threat of little immediate significance, and if, a day later, you ask them, "When is the sun due to burn out?" researchers have the hunch that a person inclined to unproductive obsessing would instantly reply, "7.5 billion years!" and someone not so inclined would reply, "A very long time from now — I can't quite remember."

David A. Clark writes in *Cognitive-Behavioral Therapy for OCD*, "[Researchers] compared patients with OCD and non-clinical individuals (controls) on their ability to forget or remember a list of threat words, positive words, and neutral words. The OCD group . . . had greater difficulty forgetting threat words relative to positive or neutral words, as evidenced by significantly greater recall and recognition of the threatening 'forget' words." The jury remains out as to whether part of the difficulty in turning off obsessions, productive or unproductive, is our inability to forget a perceived threat, but the hypothesis is tantalizing.

Maybe the half-conscious memory of your last business failing prevents you from letting go of your current business obsession, to the extent that you're exhausting yourself and making yourself ill. If so, you need to forget about that past business failure. Maybe remembering that your first two novels haven't sold operates as a threat preventing you from fully investing in your current literary obsession and leading you to obsess instead about whether your current novel will be marketable. You need to forget about those two unsold manuscripts.

It is easy to imagine how "threat awareness" might be implicated in our overobsessing or unproductive obsessing and how "appropriate forgetting" might be the answer. As part of your practice, ask yourself, "Is there some threat that I need to forget in order to stop obsessing?" That threat may be lurking in a corner of your awareness, and by asking yourself this direct question you may be able to spot it and show it the door.

chapter twenty-seven

Turning Your Productive Obsession Back On

MAYBE YOU SHUT DOWN YOUR PRODUCTIVE OBSESSION be-cause you had to pay focused attention to the rest of your life. Maybe you shut it down because you encountered some problem — a plot problem in your novel, a technical problem in your research. Maybe it petered out of its own accord. At some point you will need either to turn your productive obses-sion back on or to nurture a new one. You do not want to go too long without a productive obsession in place, since that will mean that you won't really be thinking.

The main stumbling block to turning your productive ob-session back on will be a negative relationship to the very idea of productively obsessing. Productive obsessing will prove that much harder if you aren't comfortable with the idea of pro-ductively obsessing. For some people, biting into an idea and pursuing it for weeks, months, and years on end has been their style since childhood. Maybe they wrote a novel at nine or launched an Internet business at thirteen. Most people, however, did not manifest this style in childhood and may be coming to this practice for the first time only now. If this process is new to you and consequently doesn't "feel" like you, you may find it hard to reengage with it.

Consider the following report from Marcia: "I've realized that I am not usually an obsessive person and that my personality seems to fight against obsession, so for me this was a new concept. Nevertheless my obsession is growing slowly. I tend to do everything at a slow pace, which is another personality pattern, but I've become more diligent in my efforts. Projects that I've been procrastinating about for years are beginning to get done. I'm working at my art, not just dropping it or putting it on a back burner. I like this. I like the feeling of being committed to my projects. I like the fact that I'm seeing results. Maybe this is my comfort level with obsessing — or maybe I'll get even more obsessive. Only time will tell. In the meantime I am very pleased."

You may have a strong philosophical aversion to the idea of productively obsessing: you may believe that you should live in balance, define balance as getting neither too excited nor too down, and see productive obsessing as unwanted excitement. You may have a strong psychological aversion to the idea of productively obsessing: it may trigger long-standing injunctions against really trying or against speaking in your own voice. You may have a cultural aversion to the idea of productively obsessing: it may have been drummed into you that your brain is not really at your own disposal but must be used for group purposes. These are real obstacles to overcome. The first step in restarting your productive obsession is keeping an open mind about the process and buying into the idea that productive obsessing will serve you.

John, an artisan baker and practicing Buddhist, gave productive obsessing a fair try and reported at the end of two months: "I've been working for years learning how to detach. So the idea of cultivating productive obsessions made me nervous. There was something so contradictory about emptying my mind and also creating large neuronal gestalts of long duration that I just about dismissed the whole thing out of hand. But I had the nagging suspicion that there was more to getting a grip on my mind than just learning how to empty and detach. It seemed to me that emptying and detaching were starting points, not end points, and that you engaged in those practices in order to get your mind in the right place to do lots of interesting work. The more I thought about it, the more I could see how the two might not be antithetical.

"I actually knew what I wanted to obsess about — I wanted to obsess about 'traveling not as a tourist.' I had the gift of a significant chunk of time approaching, and I wanted to use it in some interesting way. I knew that I wanted to travel, but beyond that I didn't know what I was thinking. Many clichés popped into my head — I could visit Zen monasteries in Japan, I could trek the Himalayas or the Andes, I could study with a Zen master in Korea, I could study with a master baker in France — but none of these seemed like my own idea. Each was reasonable and even attractive — and yet fell short. So I set myself as my starting point the question, 'How can I travel well, not as a tourist and not in somebody else's footsteps?' I loved my question — but found the first weeks of productive obsessive really frustrating.

"It made me almost physically sick to try to obsess when I

had spent so much time over the years learning to empty my mind. After about two weeks, I threw in the towel. But that didn't sit quite right with me, so I made myself the deal that I would try one more time. I posed myself my question, went for an early-morning walk, and allowed myself to fill up with images and ideas. For whatever reason, this time the process felt less scary and disorienting. Suddenly I landed on the image of a small bakery in Italy stocked with all sorts of rolls. I realized that I loved rolls — and that I had never paid them enough attention. This would be my obsession!

"Then I had to decide what I meant — would I focus on one region of Italy, all of Italy, or maybe Italy, France, and Spain? And what did 'focus' mean? Would I keep a journal, blog about my adventure, think about writing a book, or what? To make a long story short, by the end of a month of obsessing on my 'roll voyage' I had the trip planned and, more than that, I had a vision of what the trip meant. Whether I'll be traveling with an empty mind or an obsessive mind remains to be seen. But I'm glad that I turned my obsession back on after nervously shutting it down."

GRACED WITH AN OBSESSION

Sondra Barrett, who began her professional life focusing on the molecular makeup of leukemia cells in children, has spent decades photographing images of molecules as seen under the microscope. Barrett, who has a PhD in chemistry, fell in love with molecular imagery and was amazed to find that photographed molecules not only were beautiful but often seemed to mimic the molecule's effect on humans. For example, caffeine molecules appeared with jagged edges, and cortisol, the stress hormone, looked as menacing enlarged as it feels when excessively running through your system.

In the mid-eighties, Barrett was given the opportunity to study winemaking, which, she reports, brought together her "three passions: science, art, and wine." She writes, "You could say that I fell in love with wine from the inside out. Creating photographs of wine became an unexpected obsession of mine." In the twenty-five years since learning that photographing molecules using an "interference" microscope added real meaning to her life, Barrett has created a professional path that manages to marry her many interests. Today she teaches and practices in the new field of psychoneuroimmunology (PNI), a branch of body/mind medicine, and she completed her first book, *Wine's Hidden Beauty*, in 2009.

By pursuing her passions, Barrett had several obsessions grace her, including one with molecular wine imagery that she couldn't have anticipated when she first looked through a microscope. You too may love something but may not have had the perfect obsession grace you yet. If you keep your eye on your love, maintain your interest, and hold yourself open, how can it not grace you eventually?

chapter twenty-eight

The Glory of Brainstorms

PRODUCTIVELY OBSESSING IS A HABIT OF MIND that you initiate and nurture. It is a simple habit to describe: you enlist your brain in the service of matters that interest or concern you. *Enlist* may be the wrong word; *draft* may be more appropriate. Your mind may prefer its habitual ways and opt for fear, fantasy, worry, regret, or idleness rather than intense and systematic thinking. So you may have to draft it into service and send it through boot camp.

Military boot camp normally lasts for a few months and is followed by several more months of learning a specialty. There is a reason for this. New habits take time to learn and often require the watchful eyes (and loud mouths) of drill instructors. Before commencing basic training you are warned not to bring pets, cameras, radios, magazines, newspapers, playing cards, dice, or anything else that might distract you. For those months you are meant to focus; by the end of that time, having focused, you may be a different person.

Productive obsessions deserve this sort of commitment and attention. Our brainstorms, as we birth our novella, build our foundation, or solve an everyday problem, are the brain's glory. You do not have an idea for a movie and in the next instant possess the actual movie. For that movie to exist in reality, your brain has to embark on a genuine journey. You do not have an idea for a new way to do business and in the next instant possess an up-and-running company. For that company to exist in reality, your brain must work as hard as any locomotive. All that glory is available, but you will have to work for it.

It is hard to attach a word like *glory* to the boring-seeming image of a scientific researcher sitting at a monitor poring over computer simulations, a poet scratching out ten words for every two she keeps, or an administrator plotting how to keep her nonprofit's footing in a hostile country. Watching these individuals do real and important work is about as exciting as watching paint dry, which is why thinkers are rarely celebrated in movies or chatted about at the office water cooler. You never hear anyone say, "Wow, did you see the way John sat there yesterday, thinking!" The greatest glory of our species, our brainstorms, are so boring to observe that people would prefer undergoing a root canal to watching someone think.

So we must leave visual drama out of the equation. There would be nothing interesting about watching Kafka sit behind a desk at the bank where he worked, even if he were dreaming up *The Trial*. There would be nothing fascinating about observing Einstein sit behind his desk at the patent office, even if he were calculating the relationship between mass and energy. There would be nothing thrilling about spying on the Canadian painter Emily Carr as she stared at the mountain she repeatedly painted. Inside your head a glorious brainstorm may be occurring, but its external manifestation is completely boring. Do not look for outside validation, enthusiasm, or excitement as you pursue your brainstorms. You are the one who must feel enthusiasm. You are the one who must validate your pursuits.

By using your brain in an intentional, concentrated way you bite into ideas and make yourself proud. Jodie noted this self-pride in her two-month report to the productive obsession group: "One of the things that I'm doing is communicating more clearly. For example, last night I wanted to spend some time working on my Internet business. My boyfriend got home from teaching his juggling class; he eats dinner after he gets home. I was completely honest with him and told him that he needed to deal with his own dinner because I wanted to work. Once it registered that I meant it he agreed without a fuss.

"I'm also putting my work in front of me, even when I can't actually work on it, so that it becomes a part of my everyday life. Now at my day job I keep a notebook where I make notes on the business. If I have a sudden inspiration, I scrawl a note to myself. I think in some respects these are two sides of the same coin. On the one hand, I'm openly acknowledging to everyone that I've chosen to take this obsession seriously. On the other, I'm giving myself a constant reminder that I'm taking this seriously. I've never done anything in my life that has made me feel more proud."

This could have been a book about the productive obsessions of celebrated people — of painters, poets, inventors, and entrepreneurs with household names. But if they'd received any more space than the minimal space I've given them it would have distracted you from the truth that productive obsessing is available to anyone who is willing to engage in the process. You don't need to be a "natural" at obsessing; you don't need extraordinary talent or discipline; you don't need tremendous brainpower to incite glorious brainstorms. You need only the phrase *productive obsession*, with its built-in magic, and a willingness to begin.

Once this distinction is brought to people's attention, they intuitively understand the difference between productive obsessions and unproductive ones. Jennifer, a researcher, explained: "Productive obsessions are forward looking. They point to future actions like tomorrow's work or to some activity that I expect will be pleasurable and engrossing. These thoughts are characterized by feelings of competency and ability, even of power. The thoughts are outward directed, about things other than me, and lead to excitement and energy. Unproductive obsessions, by contrast, are backward looking. They chatter in the mind and are replays of bad decisions, bad experiences, and especially disasters. These thoughts are characterized by feelings of incompetence, stupidity, or powerlessness. They are all about me and lead to depression and exhaustion. The difference is clear — and now I have the language to distinguish them."

Marcia, a musician, explained, "Productive obsessions seem to be our life force. They inspire and move us forward. They are our reason for getting up in the morning. They feel joyful. True, there are times when we are also frustrated by these productive obsessions, but that passes. The frustration is usually the result of feeling that we aren't doing enough or that we are currently unable to reach the quality of work to which we aspire. When productive obsessions become our focal point, they lead us to success.

"The most significant thing about unproductive obsessions

is that you feel guilty, not good enough, that you don't measure up. They are based in fear, and we use them as tools for self-flagellation. In fact, they prevent us from moving forward and achieving our goals because of the attention we give to them. They can become our negative focal point, preventing success. I am striving to grow the one kind and eliminate the other. I don't know if I can do that, but at least I have a clear intention."

Productive obsessing is more than the way you use your brain to its best advantage. It is the way that you manifest your thoughtfulness. Embark on a month of productive obsessing, then a second month, and, ultimately, a lifetime. If you end up with a novel like *Middlemarch*, a ballet like *Swan Lake*, a business like Apple, or a new theory of relativity, congratulations. But congratulate yourself just as much if what you end up with is the experience of authentic living. If you've nurtured a stream of brainstorms in the service of heroic self-actualization, pop that champagne cork.

THE MYSTERY OF IT ALL

During my junior and senior year in high school and for a semester in college I thought I would become an astronomer. Why? Because the night sky moved me. However, I quickly learned that the scientific details of the sky did not interest me. I looked elsewhere to experience mystery. For many people, though, the night sky remains, or resurfaces, as one of their primary places of mystery. Consider, for instance, Charles Calia, whose passion for the night sky was unexpectedly reawakened while he was gazing at the stars in the presence of his two young daughters.

In middle age, Calia, a novelist, returned to his youthful love of astronomy. From that experience emerged *The Stargazing Year*, in which he chronicles twelve months spent enraptured by nighttime skies and his attempt, begun in the dead of a Connecticut winter, to build his own backyard observatory. *The Stargazing Year* weaves together Calia's building escapades, his night-sky observations, constellation mythology, and familial interactions. It is not a year of astronomical breakthroughs — no new planets are discovered, no new comets are named — but rather a year of joyful participation in mystery.

A brainstorm is creativity in action and problem solving in action, but it is also a gathering into mystery, a journey by neurons and not by starlight. As we travel to those mysterious reaches, we are mirroring the journey that millions of our best and brightest have undertaken when they fired up their neurons and sat back, thinking. They went through what we will go through: all those bumps, bruises, and glory. Those who follow us, when they decide to bite into an idea and create a brainstorm, will smile in our direction — at their cherished ancestors. All those brainstorms constitute the history of thought.

appendix

Your Productive Obsession
Group

READING ABOUT MY PRODUCTIVE OBSESSION GROUP may have intrigued you, and now you may want to start a similar group of your own. Many people find group support useful, even invaluable. In a well-functioning group, members report on their ups and downs, learn from one another, celebrate successes, and feel "in it together." Because productively obsessing can be a challenging habit to acquire and because false starts often precede solid obsessing, having group support and accountability available can keep people "in the game" during what may be the difficult early stages of their obsessing adventure.

If you want to launch a group of your own, here are some guidelines for starting, maintaining, and ending your group.

1. Think through the sort of group you want to create. Do you want a small, intimate group? If you create a small group of only

five or six people, there's the real danger that when and if some group members vanish your group will collapse. Do you want a very large group, one as large as my cyberspace group that has ranged in size from 150 to 200 members? Large groups provide a lot of interesting material and take the burden off individual members to interact a lot. But intimacy and energy can be lost, and it can prove difficult to find such a large number of participants. Probably between eight and a dozen makes for a nice-size group, small enough to be intimate and large enough to handle dropouts without collapsing.

2. Will it be a cyberspace group (that is, one that keeps in touch via email), a group that meets in an actual physical location, or some combination of the two? In my experience, no particular intimacy or warmth is lost if the group operates and interacts only in cyberspace, but you may prefer that your group meet in actuality. If that's your preference, you will need to deal with the mechanics of finding locations, coordinating schedules, preparing agendas, and so on. You may also discover that prospective participants claim that they want to meet in person — and then apologize that they can't meet at any of the times you propose. Cyberspace groups eliminate those chores and difficulties. If you want a bit more human contact, you can add audio and/or visual conference calls to your email work together. Then, however, scheduling problems once again arise; so if you prefer to avoid all scheduling challenges, keep the group email-based.

3. With the explosion of social media options, there are countless services you can use to support your group and multiple ways that your group can keep in contact. I create free Yahoo

groups for all my cyberspace purposes, groups that take only a few minutes to create and that come with a variety of useful options, among them a group website, the ability to upload and house files and photos, and a place to archive group messages. As with any affinity group, you will have to make decisions about who, in addition to you, can moderate the group, whether messages pass through the filter of a moderator or go directly out to group members, whether off-topic conversations will be permitted, and so on.

4. You will need to explain the group's purpose to prospective members. Explain to them the basic idea of productively obsessing and indicate that you'll be inviting them to try their hand at naming, choosing, and maintaining productive obsessions, either for a specific amount of time — one month, two months, or three months, say — or in an open-ended way. You might draw from this book by way of explaining the group's purpose or you might suggest to prospective members that they read this book to help them decide if they want to embark on this adventure. Let prospective participants know that the main goal of the group is to have participants come to a personal understanding of the process of productive obsessing and feel supported as they engage in that process.

5. Be the leader. Even leaderless groups have leaders, if only for a given day or for a given activity. You can rotate leadership or share leadership, but someone needs to hold the group energy, mind practical matters, and keep the group functioning. In the beginning, that probably should be you. Someone needs to remind group participants to keep their email messages on point,

to engage in personal conversations off to the side, and to get their assignments in if it is an assignment-oriented group. You will probably also need to be the person who sets the group's agenda: Will there be daily or weekly check-ins? Will there be exercises (either ones that you provide, that group members provide, or that you draw from this book)? Will there be lessons (again, either from you, the group, or this book)? All this work must fall on somebody's shoulders.

6. Have a rough plan. What do you envision happening? Are you asking group members to actively participate, perhaps by checking in on a daily or weekly basis, or do you envision having members post only when they have a question, concern, or piece of news? Are you the one who responds to these questions and concerns, or is it up to all group members to respond to one another — which may mean, of course, that no one steps up to respond to a given question or concern? Will people introduce themselves to the group? If so, do you want to create a standardized format for those introductions? Is the group a closed one, can new members join at selected times (say, at the end of the group's first two months), or can they join whenever they like? Will you provide occasional prompts and exercises, regular prompts and exercises, or no prompts or exercises? If you want to change how the group is operating — if, say, you think that you ought to change from a closed group to an open group — will that be an executive decision or a group decision? Think these matters through.

7. Actually start the group. Pick a starting day and begin. Here is the introduction that I sent out to the folks who joined my group:

Hello, everybody:

Thank you so much for joining the productive obsession (PO) group. I hope you will gain something important from learning about, generating, and making use of your own productive obsession(s).

This is a Yahoo group. You can send a message to the group by using our group email address. You can also hit "reply" to send messages to the group, since reply messages go to all group members and not just to the sender. I am moderating all group messages, so we shouldn't have much trouble with spam.

The group will doubtless generate a lot of messages, so if that begins to bother you, you can change your group setting from its default position, which is that you get every email sent, to either getting a daily digest of messages or reading the emails at the site. But I suggest that you don't make any changes for a while, since I think you will enjoy seeing what your fellow participants choose as their productive obsessions and hearing about their progress. Try to enjoy rather than be disturbed by the amount of mail we generate!

Please play by the following rules:

- Use the subject lines I suggest. That will allow people to follow threads and only open the emails that interest them.

- Have private conversations with your fellow participants privately. You may well discover that some folks in the group are very interesting to you and that you would love to keep in touch with them. Please do that privately.

You can now introduce yourself to the group, if you like. Please use as your subject line "Your Name — Introduction" (that is, "Eric Maisel — Introduction"). Introduce yourself as briefly — just a quick hello — or at as much length as you like. I will send out a long message later today explaining our first step — choosing your productive obsession for the month of May. For now, let me just welcome you. Welcome!

Best,

Eric

8. Cheerlead. Try to keep your "own stuff" out of the group by, for example, not complaining about how hard you find it to manage the group or to productively obsess. As leader and group creator you are not like the other participants, in that you need to monitor your posts a bit more than other participants do, since you want to set a positive tone, cheerlead, and keep the group's hopes and energies up. This isn't to say that you can't be human and genuine, but you do want to act a bit more like a coach than like one of the players. This is a service that you are performing for the sake of the group: making the group a happier and safer place than it would be if you were whining and complaining.

9. Respect process. To cheerlead doesn't mean that you put on a smiley face and act like the unavoidable can be avoided. Process really is process: one group member may take months to settle on her productive obsession; another may settle on his instantly and hate his choice two weeks later; a third may love her choice,

really bite into it, and discover that while she loves it she is not equal to it. The group will report many frustrations and difficulties, and these frustrations and difficulties do not need to be sandpapered away. Simultaneously cheerlead and be real.

10. Provide for check-ins. I suggest that you build check-ins into the group process. Here are two examples of the check-ins that I use:

> Hello, everybody:
>
> If you can spare a moment, please provide a three-week check-in. Here are two prompts for your check-in, if you'd like to use them.
>
> • Has your productive obsession taken hold? If not, what do you think happened?
> • What have you learned about productively obsessing?
>
> Best,
> Eric

> Hello, everybody:
>
> We are approaching the end of our first month. I hope that you will provide a one-month check-in over the weekend, since your check-ins will prove really valuable to everyone as we get a rounded sense of how this worked or didn't work for people.
>
> I invite you to try again productively obsessing in June. I will post some new guidelines and hints to help with that in a few days. Begin to think about whether or not you want to continue with and recommit to this adventure.

Please post your one-month check-in over the weekend. Post in any manner you like, but here are two questions to help you organize your thoughts. Use them if you like or post in your own way.

1. What surprised you (positively and/or negatively) about trying to productively obsess for a month?
2. What have you learned about productively obsessing that will help you make your second month of productive obsessing more fruitful?

Best,

Eric

11. Provide some small exercises. If group participants are busily obsessing, they do not need to be interrupted by you and asked to engage in an exercise. But it's more likely that many members will be struggling a bit with their productive obsessing and will relish the occasional exercise to help them get on track and stay on track. To meet the needs of both those who do not want exercises and those who do, frame the exercises as optional. Here is one of the occasional small exercises that I provide:

Hello, everybody:

It is April 30. Our month of productive obsessing begins tomorrow. Let us get some energy and enthusiasm up by having everyone post an affirmation or battle cry. Shoot off an email to the group right now with your name and either "affirmation" or "battle cry" in the subject line and then your affirmation or battle cry in the body of the email. This would look like (for example):

Subject line: "Eric — battle cry"

Body of email: "Let's go!"

Shoot yours right off to the group.

Eric

12. Deal with issues. If one person is proving to be a problem, have a private chat with that person. If the group energy is very low, address that with the group and ask for suggestions, or provide a shot in the arm with a prompt or exercise. If you are losing interest in moderating the group or feel too burdened by moderating, ask for a volunteer moderator to take over your duties for some specified amount of time, say, for a month. If people are mostly complaining, prepare and post a message of hope, an exhortation to renewed effort, or some message that helps aim them back in the direction of productive obsessing. Many issues come up in life and in the life of a group — learn to deal with them expeditiously and directly rather than ignoring them and letting them fester.

13. Have participants recommit. If you've created a time-bound group, where folks come aboard for, say, two months, at the end of the two months you'll want to invite them to continue (if you are wanting to continue). Even if the group is open-ended, you may want to get a recommitment from folks if you are sensing that energy is flagging. Here is what one of my invitations to continue looks like:

Hello, everybody:

We are at the end of our first two months together. Thank you for your participation, and I hope that you've found it useful.

For those of you who would like to continue, our third month starts tomorrow. I will post a file to the site in the next few days that combines some of the lessons I've offered so far and provides some new material. If you'd like to continue, I suggest that you take a look at that file when it gets posted (I'll send the group a message that it has been posted).

If you're continuing, please post your third-month commitment. Use as your subject line "Your name — month three." In your post, let us know what your productive obsession is/will be and your intentions for the month.

Cheers,
Eric

14. Close the group. The time may come when you decide that you are no longer interested in leading the group or when you feel that the group has dwindled in energy to the point that it no longer makes sense to continue. In the first case, ask the group if someone wants to come forward and take over the lead. If someone does, effect a graceful transition. If no one does, thank the group, wish it well, and end it. If you are closing down the group because it has lost energy and purpose, pick some group highlights to headline and use those in your exit message, in which you thank group members for their participation and wish them well.

If you have any questions, or if you would like to tell me about your productive obsession group, please drop me an email at ericmaisel@hotmail.com.

Notes

Chapter 1. The Logic of Brainstorms

Page 3: *"I think and think for months and years..."*: Hal Urban, ed., *Life's Greatest Lessons* (New York: Fireside, 1992; reprint, 2003), 152.

Page 4: *"Thoughts lead on to purposes..."*: Tryon Edwards, ed., *A Dictionary of Thoughts* (Detroit: F. B. Dickerson, 1908), 114.

Page 5: *"after a decade of digging through old graveyards..."* and *"some of the borough's earliest settlers..."*: Sarah Kershaw, "Protector of the Long Departed; Historian Restores Early Burial Plots in Queens," *New York Times*, December 27, 2000, www.nytimes.com/2000/12/29/nyregion/protector-of-the-long-departed-historian-restores-early-burial-plots-in-queens.html (accessed March 8, 2010).

Chapter 2. Putting Your Brain into Gear

Page 9: *"Obsessions are thoughts which come to the foreground..."*: Ian Osborn, *Tormenting Thoughts and Secret Rituals* (New York: Dell, 1998), 30.

Page 13: *"exquisite geometrical intricacies"*: Buffalo Museum of Science, "Bentley Snow Crystal Collection: Wilson A. Bentley Biography," www.bentley.sciencebuff.org/Bio.htm (accessed March 8, 2010).

Page 13: *"The experience of the search for new forms..."*: Buffalo Museum of Science, "Bentley Snow Crystal Collection: Bentley's Writings," www.bentley .sciencebuff.org/BentleyWritings.htm (accessed March 8, 2010).

Chapter 3. Large Neuronal Gestalts of Long Duration

Page 17: *"She provides detailed arguments..."*: Anthony Campbell, "Susan A. Greenfield — *Journey to the Centers of the Mind: Toward a Science of Consciousness*," www.acampbell.ukfsn.org/bookreviews/r/ greenfield.html (accessed March 8, 2010).

Page 18: *"It may be objected that what I've just highlighted isn't obsession..."*: Lennard Davis, *Obsession: A History* (Chicago: University of Chicago Press, 2009), 6.

Page 19: *"to foster a dialogue about environmental conservation..."*: ArtsWestchester press release, "Hanging by a Thread," www.artswest chester.org/index.php?module=pagemaster&PAGE_user_op=view _page&PAGE_id=637 (accessed March 8, 2010).

Page 20: *"have a history"* and *"like for viewers of my work to rethink..."*: Sam Edsill, "Fiber-Artist Turns eBay Collections into Works of Art," Mental Contagion, www.mentalcontagion.com/issue86/causeandeffect.php (accessed March 8, 2010).

Chapter 4. Choosing Your Productive Obsession

Page 26: *"Her careful observations of iridescent blue morpho butterflies..."*: Kim Todd, "Chrysalis, Maria Sibylla Merian and the Secrets of Metamorphosis," www.kimtodd.net/work1.htm (accessed March 8, 2010).

Chapter 5. Making the Ordinary Extraordinary

Page 32: *Consider Ian Bernstein*: Beam Online, "Stuff about Me," www.beam -online.com/navagation/_sam.htm.

Page 32: *"I built my first robot doll out of wood scraps..."*: Fred Hapgood, "Chaotic Robotics," *Wired* 2.09, September 1994, www.wired.com/ wired/archive/2.09/tilden.html (accessed March 8, 2010).

Page 32: *"And we might not get all of them back"*: Paul Trachtman, "Redefining Robots," *Smithsonian*, February 2000, available at www.thefree library.com/Redefining+Robots.-a071199273 (accessed March 8, 2010).

Chapter 6. Productive = Work

Page 39: *"I'm not ruling it out..."*: Jenny Shields, "One Man's Obsession, Scaling Down History," *Daily Mail*, October 31, 2003.

Chapter 7. Are You Conflicted?

Page 45: *"In order to become pathogenic..."*; *"One side of the personality stands for certain wishes..."*; and *"An effective decision can be reached..."*: Robert Dilts, "Resolving Conflicts with NLP," NLP University website, www.nlpu.com/Articles/artic11.htm (accessed March 8, 2010).

Chapter 9. Creativity and Productive Obsessions

Page 59: *"each building, furnished according to its use..."*: Nathan Moehlmann, "Cabin Fever," *Our State* 173, no. 5 (2005): 198–99.

Chapter 10. Meaning and Productive Obsessions

Page 65: *"the radio program* Flotsam Hour..."*: Flotsametrics and the Floating World, "About the Authors," flotsametrics.com/author.php (accessed July 17, 2009).

Chapter 11. Your Productive Obsession Checklist

Page 72: *English-born Captain Hutchinson*: "He Helped Ships Find Their Way: Captain William Hutchinson," ww.arkas.com.tr/english/pages/arkas_news/mart_2006/haber6.html (accessed March 8, 2010).

Chapter 12. Early Daze

Page 78: *"shadowing Laroche and exploring..."* and *"learned the history of orchid collecting..."*: www.susanorlean.com/books/the-orchid-thief.html (accessed March 8, 2010).

Chapter 13. Risk

Page 83: *"cantata of the sacred and profane"*: "A Foreword," www.david deltredici.com/alice-foreword.html (accessed March 8, 2010).

Chapter 14. Commitment

Page 89: *"Looking at the Herculean effort..."*: C. R. Jayachandran, "Japanese Guide to Indian Wonders," *Times of India*, September 6, 2003,

timesofindia.indiatimes.com/india/Japanese-guide-to-Indian-wonders
/articleshow/168720.cms (accessed February 23, 2010).

Chapter 16. Mere Interest or Passionate Interest?

Page 101: *"A more special interest I've developed over the years..."* and
"Ophrys tenthredinifera, *the sawfly orchid...*": "Behind 'The Magus,'"
Twentieth Century Literature 42, no. 1 (Spring 1996), 58–68.

Chapter 17. Two-Week Reports

Page 110: *"an appealing and genuine maverick..."*: *Kirkus Reviews* on *The
Emperor of Scent,* available at www.chandlerburr.com/newsite/
content/emperorofscent/more.php (accessed March 9, 2010).

Chapter 18. The Turmoil — and Calm — of Process

Page 115: *"Stephan Müller collects typefaces..."*: Hannah Booth, "Profile:
Stephan Müller," *Design Week,* September 14, 2006, www.designweek
.co.uk/news/profile-stephan-müller/1124407.article (accessed
July 17, 2009).
Page 116: *"Lineto and its designers were players..."*: Marius Watz,
Generator.x, "If You Love Type, Just Say Lineto," www.generatorx.no/
20051214/lineto/ (accessed February 25, 2010).

Chapter 19. Three-Week Reports

Page 122: *In 1912 the German scientist Karl Ritter von Frisch*: "Waggle
Dancing Bees," Scienceray, scienceray.com/biology/waggle-dancing
-bee (accessed March 9, 2010).

Chapter 20. Unproductively Obsessing

Page 128: *"that there is an automatic..."*: Ian Osborn, *Tormenting Thoughts
and Secret Rituals* (New York: Dell, 1998), 168.

Chapter 22. Obsessing in the Middle of Things

Page 139: *"took over"* and *"the world in which we live"*: Roger Tory Peterson
Institute of Natural History, "Biography," www.rtpi.org/
biography.html (accessed February 24, 2010).

Page 139: *"not once, when I would bring him a bird's nest . . ."*: *Birder's World* magazine, "Field of View: An Interview with Lee Peterson," bwfov .typepad.com/birders_world_field_of_vi/2008/08/lee-allen -peterson-is-the-younger-son-of-field-guide-king-roger-tory -peterson-and-his-second-wife-barbara-lee-grew-up-in.html (accessed February 24, 2010).

Page 139: *"just passing through"*: Douglas Carlson, *Roger Tory Peterson: A Biography* (Austin: University of Texas Press, 2007), 175.

Chapter 23. Journeys and Not Destinations

Page 144: *"I knew that chapter three [of* Middle Passage*] needed . . ."*: Naomi Epel, *Writers Dreaming: 26 Writers Talk about Their Dreams and the Creative Process* (New York: Vintage, 1994), 120–21.

Chapter 24. Productive Obsessions and Critical Thinking

Page 151: *"Fish, birds and furry little beasts abound . . ."*: Richard Cork, "An Irrepressible Obsession," *New Statesman*, September 27, 2004, www.newstatesman.com/200409270040 (accessed March 9, 2010).

Chapter 25. The Persistence of Productive Obsessions

Page 157: *"a structure whose name is a touch of accidental poetic truth . . ."*: Tennessee Williams, *The Glass Menagerie*, 5th ed. (New York: New Directions, 1999), 3.

Page 157: *"fifteen kids for burns"*: Tennessee Williams, *Summer and Smoke* (New York: Dramatists Play Service, Inc., 1978), 10; *"spring up with a shocked cry"*: Ibid., 9; *"There ought to be an ordinance passed . . ."*: Ibid., 10.

Chapter 26. Turning Your Productive Obsession Off

Page 164: *"[Researchers] compared patients with OCD . . ."*: David A. Clark, *Cognitive-Behavioral Therapy for OCD* (New York: Guilford, 2004), 77.

Chapter 27. Turning Your Productive Obsession Back On

Page 170: *"three passions: science, art, and wine . . ."* and *"You could say that I fell in love with wine . . ."*: Sondra Barrett, "Wine's Inner Beauty," *The World of Fine Wine* 19 (2008), 95.

Chapter 28. The Glory of Brainstorms

Page 176: *From that experience emerged* The Stargazing Year: Review of *The Stargazing Year* by Charles Laird Calia, *Kirkus Reviews* 73, no. 7 (April 2005): 395(1), available at www.allbusiness.com/retail-trade/ miscellaneous-retail-miscellaneous/4924339-1.html (accessed February 4, 2009).

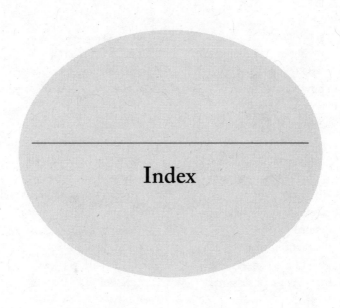

Index

About the Authors

Photo by Tiffany Lieuw

ERIC MAISEL, PHD, is the author of thirty books and widely regarded as America's foremost creativity coach. He trains creativity coaches nationally and internationally and provides core trainings for the Creativity Coaching Association. Eric is a columnist for *Art Calendar* magazine and is currently building the fields of meaning coaching and existential cognitive-behavioral therapy (ECBT). His books include *Coaching the Artist Within*, *Creative Recovery*, *Fearless Creating*, *The Van Gogh Blues*, and a score of others. He lives in the San Francisco Bay Area with his family. His websites include www.ericmaisel.com and www.brainstormthebook.com.

ANN MAISEL is a former librarian, English teacher, and school administrator who is now engaged in researching the productive obsessions of historical and contemporary figures. She